FRITZ HÄBER

THE COMPLETE DIARY

FRITZ HÄBER

THE COMPLETE DIARY

16 MONTHS IN AN AMERICAN POW CAMP

Foreword by Björn Krondorfer
Translation by Albrecht Classen

Compiled by

BERND HÄBER

MANY**SEASONS**PRESS
Mesa, Arizona • 2024

FIRST EDITION

Fritz Häber - The Complete Diary
16 Months in an American POW Camp

Copyright © 2024 Bernd Häber

Published by Many Seasons Press
123 N. Centennial Way, Suite 105
Mesa, Arizona 85201
480-939-9689 | ManySeasonsPress.com

Book Project Website: 16monthsaspow.com

Book cover design concept: Kellen Vu

Paperback ISBN: 978-1-956203-42-4

Library of Congress Control Number: 2024931710

DEDICATION

In memory of my father, Herbert Häber (eldest son
of Fritz), who passed away in April 2020.

To my wife Geneva and my daughter Helena.

To Nancy,

Thank you for your interest in my grandfather's life story.

let's not wait until history render judgement

Bernd Häber
6/9/24

TABLE OF CONTENTS

ONE HAS ALWAYS A CHOICE

ON JANUARY 3, 1933 – JUST A FEW WEEKS BEFORE THE THEN German President Paul von Hindenburg names Adolf Hitler as chancellor of Germany, my great-grandmother Meta Häber (mother of Fritz) writes in her diary: "Today is demonstration by communists. All are there, except Hanne and Anna. Hulda writes that they also voted for the communists. *Therefore, they cannot blame one another.*"

Acknowledgements

AS THE PUBLISHER OF THE DIARY, I WOULD LIKE TO EXPRESS MY heartfelt gratitude for their special support of this project to:

Björn Krondorfer - Director of the Martin-Springer Institute at Northern Arizona University and Endowed Professor of Religious Studies in the Department of Comparative Cultural Studies, for contributing the Foreword, for his valued advice on this book project and his endorsement.

Albrecht Classen - University Distinguished Professor and Director of Undergraduate Studies at the Department of German Studies at the University of Arizona for translating the original German diary into English and for his endorsement.

Hans Häber and **Uwe Häber** - for their letters and for providing related photos and documentation from family archives.

Geneva Häber and **Helena Häber** - for their feedback and guidance and for reviewing, commenting on, and proofreading all parts of the English version of the diary.

Kellen Vu - for designing the initial book front cover.

FOREWORD

HISTORY TOLD THROUGH FAMILY ARCHIVES OFTEN COMPLICATES the past. This is all the truer when descendants come across various forms of testimonial evidence of a bygone time – be it a photograph, an object, postcards, official documents, a diary – and they then commit to the thorny task of making sense of those personal remnants within the context of a larger historical framework. Such endeavor gets further complicated when family stories are situated within a violent past, for it is in these circumstances that descendants are often tempted to explain the lives of their family to the point of exonerating them of any *Mitschuld*. This is especially true for those who belong to societies that perpetrated crimes, that is, for those who need to account for the choices of family members who had supported, participated in, benefitted from, or somehow been implicated in a regime that committed grave harms against other people. We can think here of white South Africans with regards to apartheid, of the French with regards to their colonial violence in Algeria, of Russia with regards to the Gulag, of the United States with regards to the legacies of slavery and lynching, of the Turkish nation state with regards to the Armenian genocide...and the list goes on and on.

The German term *Mitschuld*, which I mentioned above, references of course the specific context of Nazi Germany, World War II, and the Holocaust. This is the setting within which the diary of Fritz Häber is situated. *Mitschuld* is an intriguing post-1945 term that suggests a certain amount of moral accountability for having lived in a criminal, totalitarian system, though such accountability remains below the threshold of legal culpability. Literally translated as something like "guilt with" or "co-guilt," *Mitschuld* might be best understood in an English-speaking context as "shared guilt." Germans born after 1945 have struggled with the inheritance of a shared collective guilt, first by employing highly politicized views to differentiate themselves from the Nazism of their parents (the 1960 generation), and then, since the late 1980s, by engaging in more personal ways to make sense of their family histories.

Many of those efforts made it into print. Though some of the publications are attempts at exonerating one's family from any moral, legal, and criminal guilt regarding the Nazi past, most second-generation authors approached the complicated task of *Vergangenheitsbewältigung* (coming to terms with the past) in more critical ways.[1] Adopting an ethical perspective regarding one's family's legacy requires to take a stance against family lore, against attempts at rendering one's family 'innocent.'[2] Literary scholars have called this genre *Väterliteratur*, literally "literature of the fathers." It refers to second-generation Germans taking account of their fathers' involvement in Nazi ideology, in the military campaigns of World War II (especially the exterminationist policies in the East), and in the annihilation of European Jews and other groups deemed unworthy of life.[3] Such a generational coming to terms with German history transpired first between sons and their fathers, and later expanded to women, including mothers compromised by Nazi ideology.[4]

With respect to the generational transmission of lethal legacies, it is important to distinguish between the second generation of victim groups on the one hand (indeed, the literature by children of Holocaust survivors and on transgenerational trauma is extensive) and, on the other, the second generation of a former perpetrator society.[5] In the latter case, there is still ambiguity about what exactly has been generationally transmitted. When children (and grandchildren) present their compromised German families uncritically by claiming in their literary and biographical writings that they too are wounded by transgenerational *trauma*, it might be a subconscious desire to identify as victims, thus blurring the differences between children of Holocaust survivors and descendants of perpetrator societies. For post-1945 Germans, it might be wiser to evoke here the term *Mitschuld* to place themselves within a transgenerational chain of *guilt* rather than trauma (which, by the way, can open the door to productively engage also with "guilt feelings").

Time, however, does not stand still, and Bernd Häber's book no longer testifies to the struggles of the German second generation. Instead, it is about a third-generation German (re)discovering the diary of his grandfather. Fritz Häber had been drafted into the Nazi German army in 1941 to serve in an anti-aircraft unit near Munich; he was eventually imprisoned in an American POW camp, where he penned the diary contained in this volume.

Living in the twenty first century, Bernd's generation itself has come of age. For them, the past is still vivid in their memory and still part of the sensory experience of family life (after all, Bernd had actually tape-recorded his grandfather back in 1990); but they themselves have no longer experienced the intense emotional and identificatory struggles of the second generation regarding the Nazi past. Today, they are the parents of the fourth and fifth generations, those children for whom the dark German past has grown distant in time and space. For the new generations, it is, indeed, just that: history. Great-grandpa's story is no longer an intimately-felt family legacy.

The growing distance to Germany's dark history may raise questions: Why publish this book at this time? For whom is it written? What is its value in today's world? To answer these questions, I need to introduce a few more layers of complication.

There is, first, the issue of Fritz's political biography. Born in 1910, he belongs to those young men who came into their own in the Weimar Republic and started their professional career when the Nazis came to power. Some scholars have called this political cohort the "generation of perpetrators," a term referring to young men in the 1930s willing to advance their careers by fully or partially acquiescing to the Nazi ideological program.[6] But Fritz belonged to a working-class background and became affiliated with the German Communist movement. Arrested by the Gestapo at age 23, he spent about a year in a prison and concentration camp. Released, he became a father of six children. Despite his membership in the KPD, the German Communist Party, he was eventually conscripted into the *Wehrmacht* (German army) in 1941.

You may wonder: A working class German Communist fighting in Hitler's army? The biography of Fritz defies our expectations of how and why Germans fought in World War II, even when they opposed the regime and spent time in prison as enemies of the state. As genocide scholars have often remarked: no matter how solid a hateful ideology presents itself, just about anything is possible in genocidal regimes. Those regimes have the power to draw individuals into their ideological machinery, voluntarily and coercively, and to force individuals to make choices to the limited extent they understand their particular situation and chances of survival at the time. Is there, then, a *Mitschuld* in the case of Fritz? It is a question I would like the reader to keep in mind when perusing the diary – for it is a question that Fritz also contemplates in his own words.

Second, there is the question of cultural dislocation. By that I refer here to the fact that we have in our hands an English translation of a 1945-1946 diary originally penned in German, published in the United States in 2024. While the original diary would be understood more easily by readers in a German context, an American audience might enter unfamiliar territory with unfamiliar terminology. It may require a sophisticated reader to grasp the nuances of Fritz's descriptions and occasional political commentary. This is particularly true at a time when American political demagogues equate fascism with socialism and communism, and then package and weaponize this equation against any liberal or left-leaning policies. It might tempt some impressionable minds to read Fritz's diary as proof that communists and fascists, at the end of the day, are just the same, given that they were fighting together in Hitler's war. After all – a warped logic might ask – are not all National Socialists primarily "socialists"?

Of course, nothing is further from the truth. The fact that Fritz ended up in the German *Wehrmacht* does not demonstrate his political and personal failures but shows how Nazism used extreme coercion to terrorize and dominate individuals. In line with Hannah Arendt's analysis of totalitarianism (she writes that "total domination does not allow for free initiative in any field of life"[7]), *Fritz's story can be read as an example of how individual lives get pressed and twisted by anti-democratic, autocratic, totalitarian regimes, to the point of being hollowed out from within. When Fritz's anti-aircraft unit surrenders to the American army in April 1945, it is in the American POW camp where he, as a prisoner, confides his truer self to paper, struggling to find his own voice again.*

Third, there is the irony of history. The fact that Fritz's diary now exists in English translation is the outcome of transatlantic movements that are themselves the result of a mix of political upheavals and personal choices. Bernd, the grandson who translated the diary, grew up in East Berlin under the East German Communist government. When the wall separating East and West Berlin came down on November 9, 1989, Bernd's world radically changed. Put differently: the world opened up for him, and less than 10 years later, he left Germany and eventually settled in Phoenix, Arizona.

All of this begs the question of who is absent. It would be the son of Fritz and father of Bernd, that is to say, the so called second generation. Bernd mentions him in his introduction, Herbert Häber. Herbert had climbed up in the hierarchy of the East German Communist Party, the SED, and later became a member of the Politburo, the political body composed of the highest officials of the party, state, and security organs. In 1985, Herbert was expelled from the Politburo because of a staged high-power plot against him. Four years later, the wall was gone and East Germany dissolved. And more than a quarter century after German unification, we can now hold in our hands the diary of Herbert's father in translation. Unremarkable perhaps. Or, to the contrary, greatly remarkable given the various circumstances without which the diary could have shared the fate of so many other discarded treasures of a family archive that end up in a dump when clearing the attic.

Whatever the case might be, we can be assured of two things: for one, Fritz's diary would have been read and understood very differently in East Germany before 1989; second, without the collapse of East Germany, it would have been unlikely for the diary to be translated into English for an American audience. Somehow, we have come full circle, starting with Fritz's arrest by American forces in 1945 and leading to the translation of his diary decades later in Arizona.

These layers of history and circumstances resonate when reading the diary. It reminds me also of the unearthed family history that Konrad Jarausch pursued. The accomplished scholar of German history at the University of North Carolina at Chapel Hill published in 2011 the letters his father wrote from the Eastern front during World War II. Jarausch, too, struggled with the conundrum of how to present personal letters from the family archive in English translation to an American audience. As a German-American historian, his research had focused on Hitler's rise to power as well as on post-wall German unification and democratization. Publishing *Reluctant Accomplice: A Wehrmacht Soldier's Letters from the Eastern Front* opened a door to his family archive that he presented not only as an academic historian but also as the son of a German soldier. "Due to the cultural distance to German topics," Jarausch writes in the Foreword, an editorial choice was made to leave out a large chunk of his father's German correspondence. He calls the reader's attention to the "ambivalent role" of his father "as a reluctant accomplice," a phrasing that suggest the kind of *Mitschuld* I have mentioned above, an issue that Jarausch discusses as a "question of complicity." What is different in Konrad Jarausch's case is that he grew up without a father. His father had died in the war in January 1942. He "hovered," Jarausch writes, "like a phantom over my entire childhood."[8]

Bernd, in contrast, had a chance to meet his grandfather in person who, back in 1990 in Berlin, allowed him to read select excerpts of the diary. Even in Bernd's case, though, there remains a sense of haunting. After all, it took more than thirty years before picking up the threads and deciding to translate and publish the diary of Fritz. If ghosts can be understood as reminders of an unresolved past, their spectral presence makes itself known until we take care of them.

The diary of Fritz connects us. Bernd and I met for the first time at a public event in Phoenix in February 2020 where I presented the story of my father who, conscripted into the German *Wehrmacht* before he turned 17, spent a full year in an anti-aircraft unit protecting a German industrial complex in Upper Silesia, near a Jewish forced labor camp. Inspired by the talk, Bernd shared with me the diary of his grandfather, which led to multiple conversations regarding the viability of a publication. Later, Bernd showed me another artifact from his family archive: a hand-held fan (*abanico*) from the Spanish Civil War, signed on the back by 31 American, Canadian, and British volunteers fighting in the International Brigades against Franco's Nationalist Forces. The fan was signed in Levante (Spain) in September 1938, shortly before all International Brigadistas were asked to leave Spain and return to their home countries. Bernd had received this fan as a boy by his great-uncle (the brother-in-law of Fritz) when he was still living in East Berlin. His great-uncle had been an international volunteer in Spain, where the fan had been given to him by his comrades. This fan—a physical object of Bernd's family archive—launched a research project with students from the Martin-Springer Institute at the Northern Arizona

University. We traced and identified the names on the back of the fan through research in archives of New York and Moscow. Those names became our entry point into understanding the lives and fate of International Brigadistas in the Spanish Civil War. After two years of research and writing, we created and published a digital exhibit.[9]

Perhaps all of this leads me to say: If your relatives are still alive, talk to them. If not, do not discard quickly the stories and objects in your family archives. They might sit uncomfortably—ghost-like—in our midst, their spectral presence stored away and half-forgotten in boxes and suitcases in our attics and basements. If we allow ourselves the time to listen to them, they have much to tell us.

November 2023
Björn Krondorfer, Regents' Professor
Director, Martin-Springer Institute
Northen Arizona University

(Endnotes)

1   Here are some samples of the work by and about second- and third-generation Germans: Nea Weisberg, Jürgen Müller-Hohagen (ed.), *Beidseits von Auschwitz: Identitäten in Deutschland nach 1945* (2015); Martha Keil, Philipp Mettauer (ed.), *Drei Generationen: Shoah und Nationalsozialismus im Familiengedächtnis* (2016); Oliver Wrochem, et. al. (ed.), *Nationalsozialistische Täterschaften: Nachwirkungen in Gesellschaft und Familie* (2016); Ulla Roberts, *Spuren der NS-Zeit im Leben der Kinder und Enkel: Drei Generationen im Gespräch* (1989); Harald Welzer, Sabine Moller, Karolina Tschuggnall, *"Opa war kein Nazi": Nationalsozialismus und Holocaust im Familiengedächtnis* (2002); Claudia Brunner, Uwe von Seltmann, *Schweigen die Täter, reden die Enkel* (2004). For an Austrian perspective, see Friedemann Derschmidt, *Sag Du es Deinem Kinde! Nationalsozialismus in der eigenen Familie* (2015).

2   See Björn Krondorfer, "Abschied von (familien-) biographischer Unschuld im Land der Täter: Zur Positionierung theologischer Diskurse nach der Shoah," in *Von Gott reden im Land der Täter*, eds. Katharina von Kellenbach, Björn Krondorfer, and Norbert Reck (2001).

3   See, for example, Erin McGlothlin, *Second-Generation Holocaust Literature: Legacies of Survival and Perpetration* (2006); Ernestine Schlant, *The Language of Silence: West German Literature and the Holocaust* (1999).

4   See for example Niklas Frank's first book, *Der Vater: Eine Abrechnung* (1987; English edition, *In the Shadow of the Reich*), where he rips into the legacy of his Nazi father, Hans Frank, later followed by a similar harsh account of his mother, *Meine deutsche Mutter* (2015). For daughters and their father generation, see, for example, Barbara Cherish, *The Auschwitz Kommandant: A Daughter's Search for the Father She Never Knew* (2011), and Alexandra Senfft, *Der lange Schatten der Täter* (2016).

5   See chapter 2, "Memory: Making Choices" in Björn Krondorfer, *Unsettling Empathy: Working With Groups in Conflict* (2020), and his earlier work, *Remembrance and Reconciliation: Encounters Between Young Jews and Germans* (1995).

6   Harold Marcuse calls this generational political cohort "careerist Nazis" (*Legacies of Dachau: The Use and Abuse of a Concentration Camp*, 2001), and Gesine Schwan "Tätergeneration" (*Politik und Schuld: Die zerstörerische Macht des Schweigens*, 1997). See Björn Krondorfer, "Nationalsozialismus und Holocaust in Autobiographien protestantischer Theologen," in Krondorfer, Kellenbach, Reck, *Mit Blick auf die Täter: Fragen an die deutsche Theologie nach 1945* (2022:41-42, 56-58).

7   Hannah Arendt, *The Origins of Totalitarianism* (1976:416).

8   Konrad Jarausch, *Reluctant Accomplice: A Wehrmacht Soldier's Letters from the Eastern Front* (2011: x-xi, 1-2).

9   Martin-Springer Institute – A Fan from the Spanish Civil War (spanishcivilwarfan.org).

INTRODUCTION

W HEN I EMIGRATED FROM GERMANY TO THE UNITED STATES in 1996, I was aware of the fact that my grandfather, Fritz Häber, had been imprisoned for 16 months in an American Prisoner of War (POW) camp after World War II. He briefly mentioned it in a tape-recorded interview I conducted with him in 1990. During the interview, he permitted me to read excerpts of the diary that he had kept while he was interned.

Reading these excerpts made me want to read these chronicles in their entirety. Although more than 20 years passed before I was able to get my hands on the chronicles again, once I did, they turned out to be a fascinating read that triggered larger questions:

- How was it possible for a member of the German Communist Party – Fritz joined in 1931 – and known antifascist to serve in the *Wehrmacht*, the German fascist army, during the war?

- What was his motivation to join the German Communist Party in the first place?

- As a sincere proponent of communist ideals, why did he decide to stay put in the German Democratic Republic (East Germany) after the war and after he was expelled by the East German Communist Party in the 1950s for allegedly participating in a war crime?

As a result, I consulted my father, Herbert Häber, eldest son of Fritz, about these aspects of my grandfather's life. I also was able to get hold of the diaries of my great-grandmother Meta Häber, mother of Fritz. Both sources provided the missing pieces of my family's history that led to my decision to publish my grandfather's diary almost 80 years after he returned home to his family in 1946.

I was born in East Berlin after the Berlin Wall was erected and grew up in the German Democratic Republic. My father became a politician and was appointed a *Politbüro* member of the East German Communist Party in 1984, the highest level of political and state power in the country. In 1985, he was expelled from this body for alleged treason. Following the reunification of Germany in 1990, he was also indicted and prosecuted for allegedly having been responsible – as a member of the *Politbüro* – for some killings at the Berlin Wall.

My father's involvement in politics taught me to always look beyond the surface to dig deeper and to ask tough questions when trying to understand how government decisions impact the daily lives of ordinary people. It was hence all the more exciting to discover that my grandfather, throughout his diary, repeatedly reflected on how the political developments during the Weimar Republic in the 1920s and during the Hitler reign in the 1930s had influenced his upbringing, his life as an ordinary citizen, and his imprisonment.

Here is an example from September 10, 1945:

"Let's get to the essence of it: The military and political collapse with all its accompanying circumstances was so horrible for both the German people and us as soldiers that the majority of people stopped believing in anything. If we are to continue with such an attitude, life would not be worth living. This can't be. Hence, we need to trust and believe in the future, neither blindly nor fanatically, but following a complete reversal of our thinking, deliberate and consciously by scrutinizing ambiguity. If we all could do that while still in captivity, we will do a lot for our people. Because it is not about the one or the other individual or, even more reprehensibly, just about the ME, it is about the long-standing imperative to form a society, about all of us, and about us as the people and our continued existence as a people."

Compared to many of my fellow German countrymen, I am quite fortunate to have access to personal family documents as well as written and verbal testimony that discuss life in Germany during this time period. It has allowed me to come to terms with my family history in a surprisingly transparent manner. For decades after the war, it was an absolute taboo for many families in postwar Germany to discuss the sensitive subject of the brutal fascist German reign. While children wanted to understand what had happened, incessantly asking their parents and grandparents, many kept it a secret in fear of exposing involvement in war crimes or, at a minimum, complicity with the Nazi regime, no matter how it came about. It was only after the insistence of postwar generations that people eventually began to open up about their lives between 1933 and 1945; in some cases, this discussion initiated a healing process and gave closure to wounded souls and the conscience.

At last, I am delighted to be able to share this diary with the public because it opens a rare window into a thrilling personal account and unique perspective of World War II.

Fritz Häber – A Brief Introduction to His Life

Before 1933

As the youngest among his siblings, Fritz was born on January 22, 1910, in Leipzig/Saxony, Germany. His parents, Meta and Emil Häber, owned a laundry shop – a seasonal occupation and small business endeavor very typical at the time – that often forced them and their family to move from city to city across the state of Saxony for periods of time.

The family eventually settled in Zwickau/Saxony, where Fritz entered a vocational school in 1924 as a blacksmith apprentice, graduating in 1927. His school grade certificate reveals that Fritz was an excellent student with a high degree of studiousness across various school subjects, such as math, practical mechanics, German as a language and life skills (*Lebens- und Bürgerkunde*).

Over the course of the next three years, Fritz worked as a blacksmith at various smitheries in the region, where he earned decent wages; most of it he contributed to the family income. He also worked part-time as a mechanic in a steel mill and even as a snow shoveler for the city of Zwickau between January and March 1929 – a well-paid assignment which, regrettably, as he mourned, "literally melted away."

Between January 1930 and April 1933, Fritz experienced the hardship of long-term unemployment. He faced the challenge of finding any solid work; he worked moonlighting jobs (*Schwarzarbeiter*) and risked, if caught, losing his unemployment and welfare benefits – none of which paid enough to provide a decent living.

Otto and Kurt, his two elder twin brothers born in November 1903, had a lasting influence on his upbringing. During the 1920s, the twins became journeymen as they sought and found seasonal work as trained masons in cities across Germany, such as in Berlin, Dresden, and Cologne.

During these years, Fritz started to get involved in the Communist movement, such as when he became a member of an affiliated wrestling sports club. After joining his brothers at rallies associated with the movement protesting unemployment and the political developments in the country, Fritz became a member of the German Communist Party in November 1931.

In his diary, he states:

"In my last school year, I distributed the Communist news-paper *Der Kämpfer*. I never lacked any newspaper read-ings. My parents at that time subscribed to four newspa-pers, of which each represented the orientation of one of the larger parties. That provided me with the opportunity, in connection with observations about real life, to form my own and firm opinion. My two brothers, whose profession was masonry, had found their way to the Communist party via trade unions."

These activities and his party membership had dire consequences for Fritz since he was to be politically persecuted by the Nazis after they took reign in Germany in 1933.

1933–1946

At the age of 23, Fritz was arrested by Hitler's secret police and taken into protective custody (*Schutzhaft*) in April 1933 for allegedly assisting his brother Kurt with "conjointly preparing an undertaking of high-treasonous nature." Fritz writes in his diary:

"Around that time, one of my brothers was thrown in pris-on for the first time because he had illegally distributed forbidden Communist newspapers."

On June 9, 1933, his mother, Meta Häber, describes in her diary how Fritz was detained by the police:

"Fritz has been in police custody for 14 days. Why – one cannot find out. He was working retreading shoes when a car suddenly stopped by for them to pick him up. Before one could realize what was happening all went by so fast."

Fritz was held prisoner at the Osterstein Castle in Zwickau but was released a few weeks later, on May 4. The castle was an early version of a concentration camp that took so-called seditious elements into custody, such as Communists. As such, it was not yet a camp where mass killings would take place years later, like in Auschwitz or Buchenwald. Yet, only a few weeks later, on May 24, he was arrested again and, this time, taken into pre-trial custody (*Untersuchungshaft*). Hitler's henchmen had actually been after his brother Kurt, who was hiding in Dresden at the time; they had used Fritz as bait. The criminal charge against both brothers was nonetheless high treason (*Vorbereitung zum Hochverrat*) as the result of having allegedly supported the activities of the Communist Party of Germany.

According to her diary, Meta was kept mostly in the dark by officials about the actual charges until Fritz was released from custody one year later, on May 25, 1934, due to a "lack of sufficient evidence of guilt." Kurt, however, was found guilty and convicted. He had to serve two years in a penitentiary. It is not exactly clear to what extent Otto was involved in the activities of Kurt and Fritz. He also ended up in prison, as his mother documents in her diary in September of 1933:

"Now, hopefully all will pass mercifully. Otto will not get punished because he has been detained since March 7."

Upon his release from prison, Fritz worked mostly short-term jobs as a day laborer (*Handlanger, Montagehelfer, Hilfsarbeiter, Landwirtschaftsgehilfe, Notstandsarbeiter*) for the next two years until he secured permanent employment as a department manager (*Disponent*) at a local freight train railway agency in Zwickau in April 1936. He worked there until he was drafted as a *Wehrmacht* soldier in August 1941.

By that time, he had been married to Linda since 1935 and was a father of six children.

How was it possible that Fritz, having six children and being a member of the German Communist Party, ended up serving in the *Wehrmacht*, the German fascist army? Did he volunteer? Did he have a choice? As he documented in his diary, three attempts were made to draft him. His employer was twice able to successfully file an exemption from military service and deferment. As Fritz wrote:

> "The third time, when I got a draft order, it was over. No one in the firm could help me avoid it any longer. I personally did not care. Such a destiny that had become reality already for millions, I could no longer escape."

The war was already in full swing in August 1941. Germany had just attacked the Soviet Union in June, now facing a two-front war, and therefore, the *Wehrmacht* desperately needed soldiers. Fritz's choice, given his former run-ins with the Nazi regime, was to serve (and survive) or face imprisonment again or even execution. Fritz reflected on the leaders of the Communist Party in his diary:

> "A great number of them were eliminated during the years since 1933. Many of the others were, despite their unreliability, drafted into the military and were placed in units that suffered great losses."

Fritz ended up serving in the *Wehrmacht* as a junior commander of an anti-aircraft gun unit operating searchlights, located near Munich, that beamed at approaching Allied aircraft bombing squadrons. In the nearly one hundred pages of his diary, he also gives – in precise detail – his account of serving as a soldier, from the moment when he was drafted to the day his unit surrendered to the Americans in April 1945. While interned by the Americans as a prisoner of war (POW), he did not hear from his family for over a year until he finally received two letters from Herbert with news about their situation back home in Zwickau. As a result of his resilience, Fritz survived and returned home in August 1946.

4/45 → 8/46

After 1946

Reading his diary, we see Fritz not just reflecting on the dire circumstances of his imprisonment and the struggle to survive but also exhibiting a rational mind. His writings reveal an extraordinary character who understands and captures the larger context of the times in which he lived. On many occasions throughout the diary, he shares his worldview and analysis of how Germany turned from the Weimar Republic democracy into a fascist dictatorship:

> "Once the Treaty of Versailles was sealed, the economic impoverishment of the German people was contractually determined for years to come. This condition made it possible for the reactionary forces at the same time, by raising the deceptive question, who had been responsible for the war, to win over dissatisfied nationalistic sections of the people for their ideas. The goal of those circles was to organize a new movement, which intended to restore an old-world German dominance. In order to gain influence among the broad masses, this movement put on a deceptive cloak by way of formulating social and revolutionary demands, a movement that was supported by the high finance."

His worldview was clearly shaped by his personal life experience during the 1920s and the early years of the Nazi regime, the progressive influence of his two elder brothers, and the encouragement of his mother to get involved. Furthermore, joining the German Communist Party – contrary to the Social Democratic Party of Germany that, as one of the governing parties, had failed to protect the Weimar Republic democracy – provided the philosophical and educational framework for him to study German history and to understand the social context. His membership in an affiliated wrestling sports club prepared him for the psychological and physical challenges ahead of his imprisonment – to fight, to stay alive, and to win.

After his release as a POW in August 1946, Fritz returned home to his wife and now seven children in Zwickau. The city was now part of the Soviet occupation zone of what would become the territory of the German Democratic Republic (East Germany) in 1949. He had high expectations of which direction the postwar Communist society should go. In his diary, Fritz referred to one of the letters that he had received from his son Herbert while being in the camp in Metz in France.

> "He writes rather understandably. He is active in the Free German Youth movement. I would not have expected anything else. In my estimation, this generation and our own face a gigantic political task."

And yet, it seems inconsistent with his worldview that Fritz – as a sincere proponent of communist ideals – continued to live in East Germany, especially after he was expelled from the East German Communist Party in 1954. That year, Fritz was accused by his fellow Communist Party comrades of being responsible for the death of a fellow countryman during the war. They accused him of having, as a member of a *Wehrmacht* execution squad, killed an innocent man. Fritz briefly mentions this incident in his diary. The documented sources identifying the victim, however, vary; one source claimed he was a fellow soldier who attempted to desert his obligation to fight, and another reported that he was a French camp laborer who had stolen a loaf of bread. During wartime, both deeds were punishable by death.

As one can imagine, it was quite a sensitive subject for Fritz because the accusation felt like a stab in the back and ultimately led to the revocation of his party membership. As he found out years later, the accusation was also the result of a personal vendetta against him. My grandfather, however, did not shy away from addressing and talking about it in written statements and letters; he also talked about both the shooting squad incident and expulsion from the party during my tape-recorded interview with him.

One aspect that played a significant role in Fritz's decision not to leave East Germany and to seek residence in West Germany (before the Berlin Wall was erected in 1961) was that his eldest son Herbert had started a promising political career in 1951 at the center of state power, the Central Committee of the East German Communist Party in Berlin. This career ultimately led Herbert to become a member of the party's *Politbüro* in May 1984.

Fritz had high hopes that his son would be able to help him reverse the decision of the local party leadership and reinstate his party membership. For a variety of reasons, it did not work out this way. Coincidentally, Herbert himself was expelled from the *Politbüro* in October 1985 as a result of a staged high-power plot against him.

For decades, Fritz tried to get his expulsion from the party overturned because of a lack of social recognition from many of his colleagues and peers. It was not until 1991, following the fall of the Berlin Wall in 1989 and the reunification of Germany in 1990, that he was fully rehabilitated, politically and morally, by a resolution of the managing committee of the Party of Democratic Socialism (PDS). Fritz passed away in June 1998.

After German reunification in 1990, my father Herbert was indicted and prosecuted for being allegedly responsible, as a *Politbüro* member, for some of the killings at the Berlin Wall. He had to face two related criminal trials at the District Court of Berlin between 1995 and 2004. For the record, Herbert was able to prove his innocence. It took a very long time, too, for him to get rehabilitated.

My Decision to Publish the Diary

As Fritz's grandson, working with his diary helped me to connect the dots to other materials, like the diaries of my great-grandmother

Meta Häber, additional documents in our family's possession, tape-recorded interviews, and my personal knowledge of my father's life.

Once I got my hands on the diary a few years ago, I decided to publish it. In 1990, I convinced my grandfather Fritz to sit down at his home in Zwickau for a tape-recorded interview. I asked him mostly about our family's history. Among the stories he told, he also talked about his war experiences and his imprisonment as a POW. During the interview, he showed me records of his writing, including the diary, in which he had documented memorable episodes of his life. Though the interview recordings did not provide sufficient materials to write about his life, the reappearance of his complete diary changed the game.

My decision to publish the diary in the United States has to do with me being an immigrant who came to this country from Germany in 1996. I was born in East Germany, grew up under a one-party Communist government, and experienced the fall of the Berlin Wall in November 1989 and the reunification of Germany in 1990. I want to share this story with English-speaking readers first who are interested in German history but may often assume a West German narrative.

As the diary was written in German, I decided to get it professionally translated, under the firm guidance of keeping the translation as close as possible to my grandfather's writing style and maintaining the same order of pages. Fritz's diary, at times, interrupts the chronological flow to go back in time, when, for example, he documents his time in the military or the stations of his work life. I believe this does not diminish the reading experience at all.

I have not added nor have I removed any diary content. I deemed it all necessary to understand my grandfather's unique capturing of his life experience in the context of German history during the first half of the twentieth century. I have added maps and photos to illustrate relevant places and references in the diary. Footnotes provide proper context of specific German terms and phrases that cannot be translated, of locations, and other relevant references.

Fritz writes on the first page of his diary:

"May these lines serve my wife in the future as a compensation for the long time during which she knew nothing about my well-being, and for the children to serve as an example of how human destinies can get easily mixed up."

These lines will now remind all readers of the vicissitudes of life.

I very much hope that the story of my grandfather Fritz Häber inspires and encourages readers to become interested in their own family's history to better understand the decisions their ancestors made when facing life-changing challenges, regardless of place and circumstance.

Bernd Häber, January 2024, Phoenix, Arizona/USA

THE DIARY

NOTE TO READER: Each original diary entry page will be identified within parenthesis **( )**. Endnotes will be entered within brackets [ ].

THE DIARY

By Fritz Häber

(1) Metz, June 15, 1945

I DEDICATE THESE PAGES TO MY WIFE AND MY CHILDREN OF WHOM I hope are still alive and whom to find well when I return from captivity.

The idea to compile all my previous entries in one volume came to me in Metz. At the same time, I decided to write more in detail about the first weeks in the prisoner-of-war camp. Therefore, it will be possible for me to record what otherwise will get lost in the course of time; and what is more important, through this writing I will be able to get over the hard times with more ease.

In the beginning, I will start with those entries which I began in Stenay [1] under bad circumstances. Then follow the notes from my pocket calendar, and then I will try to cover the past period from the middle of 1944 until now in such a way as it appears to be useful for me. The paper on which I wrote at that time was primitive. Only now, as we have already reached 1946, it has become possible for me to write everything once again now on better paper.

May these lines serve my wife in the future as a compensation for the long time during which she knew nothing about my well-being, and for the children to serve as an example of how human destinies can get easily mixed up.

Friday, June 8, 1945

The make-up of this booklet already demonstrates that the circumstances under which these recordings were done are quite primitive. Nevertheless, I am glad to own this paper. A comrade who owned sufficient paper for letters gave them to me. In my little pocket-calendar, I had already put down the key dates that are relevant for my time of imprisonment. But the space in it is too limited. In addition, there is all the free time that I had to make use of **(2)** to avoid losing my mind.

Six weeks of imprisonment, filled with hunger, physical stress, and disappointment.

In my notes, I return to the last weeks before the end of the war. Since June 1944, I was stationed north of Munich, in Röhrmoos [3], near Dachau [2]. At that time, I took over the command of the anti-aircraft searchlight station in Groß-Inzemoos [3]. The crew consisted of ten privates and privates first class. Additionally, every evening we were joined by six anti-aircraft gunners. The fact that this was such a group indicated to me that not so many soldiers would remain in the post. Our post itself was in a miserable condition. There were no lights, no radios, and everything was dirty. However, within 14 days, with the help of the squad and the members of the anti-aircraft gun unit, we had fixed the station to such an extent that everyone could feel comfortable there.

When we were done with that, the first group of soldiers was transferred to the infantry and the ⁴⁴ [4]. From then on, we had a quiet time. I had with me only three soldiers and those from the anti-aircraft gun units. I also want to mention that these anti-aircraft gunners carried out their service in a rotation system of one week each. They arrived at 8 p.m. and left at 6 a.m.

At the beginning of September, I got three more soldiers from the Baden region, who had been drafted only seven days ago. They had to be trained so that they could be placed at the various posts. However, we conducted almost no training. During the harvest time, we helped the farmers. That was an advantage for us because we could get enough to eat. The work was hard at the beginning, but in the course of time we got used to it.

During the height of the harvest season, I ran the smithy owned by the anti-aircraft gunner Schwalb for 14 days, who had been wounded when he had worked on forging a barrel for crude oil and therefore had to shut down the smithy. For me, those were good days. Working at this job, I realized that I still could work in my old profession, as I was fully trained to do so. The most urgent work was to sharpen plow shares and to shoe horses.

(3) As a crowning [5] for the work that I had done during the summer and the Fall, I received numerous invitations to the various *Kirchweihfest* [6] events. That was a great opportunity to really fill up with plenty of good food. Although the coachman steers the wagon the human does the thinking [7]. That is how we would describe it. And it was the case here as well.

On the Saturday of the *Oktoberfest*, I surprisingly received the order to go to Ludwigsburg near Stuttgart to serve as a trainer for women. Instead of the delicious pan-fried meal and cake typical for the festivity, I got *Kommis* [8] and experienced restless days. On Oct. 14, 1944, I began my trip together with eleven other fellow comrades. Already during the trip, some of them discussed how to approach their task of teaching those women.

We arrived in Ludwigsburg at night and slept in the barracks. The next day we had to realize with disappointment that they had no need for us at all. Instead, we were sent off to Friedrichshafen [9]. Hence, we had to shoulder our backpacks again and off we went to our new destination. Once again, we arrived at night.

It was known to me that Friedrichshafen had been bombed repeatedly. I could witness now the effects of those attacks.

The welcome in Friedrichshafen was followed by the usual military formalities. At the beginning, no office claimed to know anything about us until a higher ranked official figured out that there was some use for us. During the drive from Munich to

Friedrichshafen, a friendship developed between two other corporals and myself, which lasted for the entire training period. I will probably come back to those two later.

Our high expectations regarding the task of training those women were already diminished the very next day in Friedrichshafen. We were placed in the station of a vacated anti-aircraft battery post. There were plenty of accommodations, but in what condition! There was no trace of any women. Hence, we 'master' trainers had to **(4)** abandon the dignity of our status and had to put on work clothes in order to fix everything, to weatherize it and to make it homelike for us. We collected and borrowed all the available tools with which it was possible to clean the entire place. Before the evening, we had gotten so far as to have fixed our own 'monk cell.' We even had something like an office. The biggest job, however, was to transform all the little sheds standing in the wider area into livable quarters and to put beds into them.

We as trainers felt sorry for the girls even before they had arrived. Most of the sheds were not water-proof and let the rainwater in. Most of the windows were broken or did not exist. For the next few days, we worked as window makers, carpenters, roofers, chimney builders - that is, in every branch of homebuilders necessary for this job. As we had often experienced in the military, the impossible was suddenly possible. One evening, finally, the girls arrived. When we walked through the camp one early morning, they gazed at us through the windows. We gazed back at them.

After the girls had received blankets and a minimum of dishes, they were divided into groups for various jobs.

For me, the time of having to work with women was a visible sign of the unsustainability of our military situation. The girls had been drafted in Zirndorf near Nuremberg without having been properly equipped, and then had been sent to Friedrichshafen. There were 300 girls. But every day some had to be let go because of physical problems and ailments. Some had arrived with great curiosity and excitement, others without any interest. Their greatest

→ official state
    labor service

irritation was that they were controlled by the RAD [10] for women with its often rather monastic regulations.

The training began according to the infamous 'air force instructions of little screws' [11]. I got a group of 35 girls to train them at the 150 centimeters anti-aircraft searchlight system.

(5) I immediately established good personal rapport with them by telling them my name, my age, marital status, and the number of my children. As to the usefulness of the technical training on how to use weapons, I told them that it was all nothing but idiocy. Nevertheless, I urged them to make an effort to memorize the essential aspects of what was required from them so that the execution of duties using the equipment would be as easy as possible. The head of our camp was a First Lieutenant, a man who lacked any understanding of female concerns and needs. He, Erich Schmidt from Berlin, had risen to his present position from the lower ranks as a twelve-pointer [12]. (arrogant braggart)

He was the typical representative of that kind of people who are subservient to their authority figures and stomp on those below them. He was assisted by a middy, the topkick, who had fought in World War I and was rather narrow-minded, and we were a group of twelve trainers, consisting of sergeants, corporals, and privates first class. Also, there was a female RAD [10] cadre in charge of the kitchen made up of one Maid Leader, five group leaders, and several other maids. The entire constellation of the personnel was such that frictions erupted naturally between both leader teams.

I myself tried to move between both sides as objectively as possible so as to avoid being torn back and forth between both sides due to the weakness of the leadership structure. In the following period situations developed that were contradictory to all military norms.

The equipment to be used for the training were specially brought in from Salzburg and Augsburg, that is, by train. The condition of the equipment during the loading and in the practical implementation proved to us, who were trained with weapons [i.e., had been experienced with the war], was that they gave proof of involuntary and obvious sabotage.

The equipment was transported under great difficulties to the various sites. Most of them were never used during the eight-week training period, quite a waste. Time passed very quickly. We experienced many problems with the accommodations and with the personal (6) and sanitary conditions that the girls had to put up with. The female leadership had mostly the same qualities as any military leadership. These women took their meals together with the girls and with us trainers at the same table.

These women were so modest that they refrained from eating their full portions. When one unexpectedly visited them at night in their rooms, they harmoniously sat together and enjoyed the best food. The girls had more trust in us than in the women leaders.

During that training period we once faced the problem of flooding on the morning of November 9, 1944. It had rained heavily for two days before. On November 8, a soldier who was incompetent as a trainer and very much lacked the qualifications as 'Gaul-Leiter' [13] to handle horse's harness, crashed with the full load, food for four days, into the creek. Everyone rushed to the site of the accident and tried to fish the bread loaves and butter out of the water. In the afternoon, we as soldiers used long poles to rescue the barrels of jam out of the creek. It rained incessantly the whole day and night. Nearly all the barracks had turned into shower stalls.

During this weather we repaired the roof of the cafeteria for the girls so that they had at least one dry room. But since the headquarter was not able to provide nails and glue with the tar paper, our efforts were in vain. The wind blew everything away again. In the morning of November 9, we trainers were woken up by a loud noise from the girls' accommodations next to our rooms. When we tried to figure out what was going on, we realized that our building had turned into an island. Water was everywhere around us. The rooms in which we lived were located below the street-level and were about to be flooded. And sure enough, it happened very soon. We barely managed to rescue our possessions. Within seconds, our sheds had transformed into a lake. Most of us found rescue on the first floor. Our commander called us outside and told us that the large barrack **(7)** was completely flooded up to the window sills and that we had to find out immediately whether all the girls were safe.

We three corporals went out and aimed for the bridge at the creek, at first rather cautiously, in order not to get wet feet. But all our caution was useless. The water got into our boots anyway. When we had reached the bridge, we were faced with the question who would dare to cross it. In order to avoid any discussions, I climbed onto the bridge which had been raised by half a meter because of the water. Once I had reached the other side, I was standing in cold water which reached up to my chest. For a moment, I almost choked my own spit, but then I moved forward. I took sturdy steps, breathed in deeply, and then I was on the other side. The current of the water was strong.

In the barracks, the situation was devastating. Pieces of clothing and gear were scattered around and floated in the water. Once I arrived in the cafeteria, I jumped onto the first table and balanced along until I reached the kitchen. There, on the top of a cabinet, was a cake that had been destined for a social gathering. First, I took a piece to try it. I was so cold that all my limbs shook, and I expected that my fellow soldiers would fetch me with a raft. But nothing of that sort happened. So, there was no alternative but to pull myself together and to jump back into the flood.

Once I had returned to our accommodations, I felt like the diver in Schiller's "The Bell" [14]. In the meantime, the sun had risen, so we could assess the damages caused by the water. The girls in the other barracks were sitting on their beds. They faced water coming from both the roof and the ground. There was no heating. The key for the shed with the coal was in the flooded kitchen. Without any hesitation, I broke the window to the kitchen and got fire materials for the girls so that they could at least dry their clothes. The other fellow soldiers tried to rescue the kitchen inventory. Most of the men were too scared, fearing for their health, **(8)** to step into the water.

Since all my clothing was soaking wet, I worked, dressed only in my canvas trouser and shirt, and barefoot, all morning. As a reward for that day's work, the girls gave me some cigarettes. By the end of the morning, the water had resided, leaving behind mud and silt. The unit commander and his staff arrived and gave good advice, but the real work we had to do ourselves. The cook, an innkeeper from Pößneck [15] in Thuringia, had in the meantime secured some Schnapps, and we happily enjoyed it in large quantities. Since I had not eaten anything, the consequence was dramatic. I woke up in the afternoon, lying in my bed. None of the fellow soldiers were present. It took a moment for me to realize what had happened to me. When I arrived in the camp, the girls laughed and told me that I had staggered through the camp, drunk, and had then fallen down. In the evening, everything was good again.

The fellow soldiers, together with the girls, had undauntedly embarked on doing the clean-up job and had managed to fix most things quite well. The heavy state of my near intoxication had been of great advantage for me. It protected me from contracting a cold. By contrast, the fellow soldiers, together with the chief commander, suffered from a serious cold afterwards. The flooding was a matter everyone in the camp kept talking about for a long time.

Then the training period came to an end. In the meantime, there had been two visits for observation purposes. Once by the commander of the battalion, and once by the commander of the 26th anti-aircraft division. As expected, everyone was completely satisfied with us. But none of those bosses remarked with one word on the miserable conditions in the camp.

The girls were then assigned to individual units. At the beginning of December, the time had arrived for us to be fully deployed. But where? That was the big question which occupied everyone's mind until the secret was revealed.

(9) We were told that we were assigned to Augsburg. Shortly before the end of the seminar on November 27, eleven of the trainers were called back to the army and thus to serve in the infantry. Suddenly, I was the only one corporal left with the 'club.' ←

Only the middy, the cook, and two privates first class were to remain at the camp. Under those circumstances we loaded the equipment on December 7. The chief commander did not assist at all because he needed to wood-turn plates as Christmas presents. It was all up to me, together with the girls, to load the equipment. We loaded it onto train cars that could not be fully opened as they were of French origin.

Together with the girls, we loaded twenty-two heavy pieces of equipment and their attachments, and yet we did not suffer any accident or injury. Only those who have done this kind of job can really understand what that truly meant. I myself had to struggle with my vocal cords for days after having uttered so many commands and shouts. Then there was only the transport of the girls to be arranged. Our chief was ordered to go to the advance unit. He was a man who was not able to organize anything on his own. He always needed someone whom he could burden with responsibilities. Just for that reason, he immediately decided to take us with him because we men could be useful during the transport of the girls.

In the afternoon of Saturday, December 10, 1944, we left Friedrichshafen and arrived at our intended destination in Eurasburg near Friedberg [16] on Sunday afternoon. The rest of the unit was supposed to get here as well. What we came upon was nothing in place for us to set up a central office. Once again, we faced a nearly impossible task. In the evening, the train arrived with the girls. I had to transport some of them with a bus to the various military posts or to posts in near-by villages. In most cases, they found accommodations in private homes because the military posts could not be used for such purpose.

(10) Such matters could have been easily identified as sabotage because the command post and the upper divisions had known long before that these posts were to be taken over by women. No one had taken care of the miserable conditions of those posts. Here, the civil population had been at work not too long ago. Everything that might have been valuable or important had been removed and transported away. <u>The girls were now supposed to make those posts livable without the help of men and without any material support.</u> The division had nothing - no dishes, no nails, no tar paper. The girls told us repeatedly that they all should be let go, since there was nothing to do for them.

I had already long ago formed a clear opinion, but I could never voice it clearly as it would have been necessary. It would not have helped the girls, and it would have endangered me. Within the military unit, I assumed the position of the intelligence gathering squadron leader. That was an important-sounding title, but it was without much backing because there was really nothing to fulfill this role. With the help of the senior leader of the squadron unit, it was possible to make the battery command post operational within three days.

It was a hard piece of work. One must imagine that I could not draw from the knowledge of the girls who had been trained as communication/telephone experts. They lacked any practical training. They hardly knew how to cut off a piece of wire with the plyer.

<u>Over and over again there was clear evidence how ridiculous it was to draft women for such purpose.</u> Let us not even talk about the uselessness of deploying them to anti-aircraft searchlight units. In every aspect it was completely clear that the only purpose for all this was for the bureaucrats at the upper echelons to hold on to their own position. <u>No one had the courage to admit publicly the utter failure of this war machinery.</u>

(11) Yet, almost everyone up there had the audacity to punish the lower ranks and even officers when they, in the realistic assessment of the conditions, did not follow the theoretical instructions or observed them only loosely. I dare to claim for myself, without exaggeration, that I did everything I could to make the girls' life bearable under those absolutely miserable conditions. When I did my control drives through the posts, it mattered more to me that the girls felt alright than that the instructions were followed. Thus, it did not take long for the commander to dislike me, especially because I tried at every occasion to defend the girls.

He wanted to compensate for the lack of the military skills and the brevity of their training by applying teaching principles, as they were common for the ordinary soldiers. He applied disciplinary punishments, imposition of curfew, and ordered entire service units to do disciplinary marches – those were his methods. He also proclaimed that the girls should get used to the cold and should get accustomed to perform their service in unheated rooms. What this might mean for the girls' health, he did not care to ask himself.

My position in the unit became untenable. Moreover, he claimed that I entertained intimate relations with one of the girls, whereupon I confronted him and demanded from him to admit his lie [*Farbe bekennen*] [17]. He was too much of a coward and did not do that; instead, he tried to pursue this in a sneaky way. The issue was in fact not about any one of the girls, but an official complaint to the field-court of the 26th anti-aircraft division.

During those four weeks in Eurasburg, I lived with the owners, the Merkel family, of a small farm in Eurasburg. I felt very much at home with those people. My duties during the first eight days took me to visit all the units. This was a pretty athletic activity; I either walked or took the bike. Almost always on rural roads. When I returned home to my accommodation in the evening, my good relationship with those people fully compensated me for the many troubles and irritations during the day.

(12) During this short time, I did not feel being a soldier but a human being among other human beings. When I had to leave to rejoin with my military unit, I felt very sad. I left with the promise to try everything to return for a visit, if possible, at all in the future. For only one more last time, I had a chance to see them again. I hope that in my future life I will have the chance to visit the family Merkel in Eurasburg many more times. We often discussed the war and its outcome. And how correctly and precisely did I predict it for them, upon risk that someone could deliver me to the gallows.

On January 10, I moved away. To some extent, with a heavy heart, to another with joy. With joy because the commander could not stand anyone around himself with a straight mind. With regret because I had invested much labor and effort into the entire camp, also because of my good relationship with the girls. I knew almost all of them by their first name and had tried hard to help many of them with their personal concerns. But, as it is in the life of a soldier, there is no place for sentimentalism and personal concessions. Here again, as so often during my military service, the saying applied to me: out of sight and out of mind.

Together with the cook Wolfram from Pößneck whom I had mentioned above, I went back to the anti-aircraft gun unit in Dachau. This time was already overshadowed by the unavoidable end of the war. It was problematic to travel by train because there were constant alarms of an imminent attack of air strikes. Instead, we used a milk transporter that went to Odelzhausen [18]. From there we took a car that drove to the Reich highway between Fürstenfeldbruck and Dachau. There we stood with our heavy gear. The signpost displayed: 8 km to Dachau. There were no vehicle, no house, and no people nearby who might have been able to help us. On top of all that, heavy snow. There was no alternative for us but to shoulder the heavy bags and to walk, taking breaks here and there until **(13)** we reached the next village.

I still see us vividly today how we toiled along the road. The backpack got heavier and heavier, and what we said at that time was not proper for everyone to hear. Just as everything eventually comes to an end, so did also this march. Once we had reached the village, we first sat down to eat something and then organized a sled. Once we were mobile, we moved forward much better. In the afternoon we arrived at the central military base. To my greatest surprise I was assigned to my previous post. There I met, as before, the two privates first class, Hagl and Buchner, and eleven of the girls. We all celebrated my return. I had brought with me everything necessary for that celebration. The cook, as the essential organizer, had not been lazy and secured food. My former farmer family hosts provided cake.

At the post they still had some Schnapps, and so we spent an entertaining evening together. For the girls the party with all that food was a delayed Christmas celebration. The next day, the serious part of life set in.

I had to take over the responsibility for the post. One of the privates first class had allowed some of the things to fall apart, which I needed to correct. At first, I hit the wrong tone, when I tried to organize our duties and services according to the rules. After I had realized my mistake, I changed my strategy and approached everything in a more relaxed manner, which worked much better. After I had returned to this post, private first-class Buchner told me that he had been called to the central command where they had questioned him about my assessment of the military and political situation.

Granted, the whole matter seemed weird to me, but I simply dismissed it. I carried out my duties more or less properly, but there were often times when I was so disgusted about the military use of women that I had to pull myself together to avoid doing something stupid. *Furlough for birth of kid #7 1-10-10*

(14) I experienced a great surprise when I received a special furlough from January 22 to 29 [19]. The reason for this was the birth of our seventh child in August of the past year. At that time, I had not received any furlough. I arrived home [Zwickau] exactly on my birthday [20] and found my wife and the children all in good health. In general, my wife had great difficulties in getting enough food and clothing for the children. My furlough passed quickly. It was very hard for me and my wife when I had to leave. It was the first time during my military service that my wife accompanied me to the train station. At that time, I told her that when I would return the next time, then there would be peace. Once I was back at my post, I had not one iota of interest left in my service. The news from the military front occupied everyone. From then on, it was no longer necessary to call one of the girls to the radio. All of them came on their own because all their homeland was the focal point of the news.

One day, when I was at the central command, the commander called me in to his office and revealed that there was a judicial trial underway against me at the field-court (*Feldgericht*) [83] of the 26th anti-aircraft division. I had been denunciated by one of the party leaders [21]. I had had a conversation with that person in June of 1944 about the developments of the war. The charge against me was that I had voiced enthusiastic support for Communist rally speeches and I had wished for our enemies to gain the victory. This was shocking news for me because that party leader had been a good acquaintance of mine.

As people had regularly stopped by our post, that man had one day asked me for a smoke. It had been easy for me to do him that favor. As a result, we had developed a friendship that also extended to our families. When one lives for a long time in an anti-aircraft gun unit, one is happy about such an opportunity. Subsequently, we had visited each other and had discussed in depth the political and military situation and had also **(15)** reflected on what the future might hold for us. It was not for me, besides the danger of doing so, to bury my opinion [22]. I told people openly about my previous political past and about my way of thinking about the future. On June 8, 1944, I left the post.

I was very unclear about the entire situation, and when the chief questioned me, I pretended to be ignorant, especially because I did not yet know who had accused me. My commander was a decent guy who had not the slightest intention to cause trouble for me. He only gave me this advice and thus just warned me.

Herewith ends the block of notes from my time in Stenay. They will be followed by the notes from Metz.

14

Sunday, July 1, 1945

From this date you can see how much time has passed during which I did not write anything. Now, I have finally time to do it again. In order to frame things, I continue with the account as I have left off above. I must admit, I felt rather uncomfortable 'in my skin' at that time. It was clear to me that if this charge was pursued by a court, I could be executed. Out of precaution I could not write anything about this to my wife. At any rate, the mail service was unreliable. I could also not talk about this with the girls in the post. During that period some of my hair turned grey. But that hair has since disappeared, which was due to the work with the girls. These were weeks filled with anxiousness.

Finally, on March 6, 1945, I was called to the field-court in Grünwald [23] for questioning. I rode a bike from Dachau all the way down there. For food, I had a piece of dry military bread with me. I arrived there on the dot at 9 a.m. I was tortured by the question of how this would end for me, and who was the denouncer, but I had to rein in my impatience until 3 p.m. This gave me an opportunity to visit Deisenhofen.

(16) There, I got close to the military post from where the denunciation had come, as I learned later. Only by accident did I not visit that suspected "party comrade". The reason was that I needed to get lunch somewhere. My travels took me to the Wallner family whom I had previously visited many times. I experienced an affectionate welcome and was well fed.

Finally, the time had arrived. On that day it had snowed heavily, and - while marching with my bike through the Grünwald forest - I started to sweat and to get nervous quite a bit. At the court, the Judiciary Major Schmucke questioned me. This finally gave me clarity about the whole situation. Through the manner in which they did the questioning, I realized that the judge was favorably inclined toward me. It did not take long and I was dismissed. I felt as if I had received my life a second time. For one thing, I was shocked that I had been denounced from that direction. Second, I finally understood where the stab in the back had come from. In my mind, I was not afraid of getting my head chopped off because I had prepared myself for that already mentally. It felt good that I was able to exchange opinions with my fellow anti-aircraft men. I wished that a bomb would drop on the field-court nonetheless. Nothing of that sort happened, but the military front approached very quickly. Some things changed at our post because the staffing of the girls had changed.

My service girls had to go to Niederroth, and the ones from there were ordered to my post. Those who had to leave felt very sorry about it, and those who arrived had mixed feelings. I had the reputation to be rather exact when it came to the details. During the first days of this exchange, I felt like a man whose wife had died. I had to train the new crew once again. We sniffed each other out without gaining mutual trust. On the first day, I had taken the gang of girls to task to follow the 'holy order' [24]. Within eight days, I had the same relationship with the new crew as with the old one. A sign of that was that the girls **(17)** called me *Herrmännel* [25]. That was a way of speech I employed with my children, and I allowed the girls to use it as well.

I could write many pages about the interactions with the girls at large. In case the imprisonment will last for a long time, I will do that, and for the simple reason that I cherish the memory of that time. As I mentioned above, the events at the military front occupied us much. Our troops had already arranged for us to be prepared to abandon our post immediately upon a code-word when the enemy forces would suddenly appear. In that case, there were plans to destroy the equipment. One early Sunday morning, we got the code-word through the telegraph. Everything had to be readily packed to be able to go to the farmers. It felt like being in the midst of a pigeonry. Everyone really wanted to just go home. It cost me all my rhetorical skills to keep them from doing stupid things.

On Sunday before Easter [12], it became more serious. We were told to be ready to receive the code-word. This condition lasted until Monday. The reason was that the Americans had suddenly moved up to Crailsheim [26]. It was hopeless to get much done with the girls. Without any delay, I therefore decided – trying to overcome their initial resistance – to paint the shed myself and promised to turn it into the best-looking one in the entire company. This inspired them to finally support the effort.

Without having any paint or any other material, we nonetheless began with the work. Improvisation was the key word for an anti-aircraft post buildup construction. We washed all the walls, we scratched off the old paint and promptly reused it.

For the base, I had organized some oil from an electric engine which had been destroyed by Mustang planes [27]. In the evening, everything was done, and the barracks were completely painted anew. For the interior decoration, I created rods for the curtains. The girls organized curtains and tablecloths. Outside below the windows we placed flower pots and planted blue lungwort. For the Easter holiday baking we had **(18)** spared some of the butter and sugar, despite our great hunger, from our sparse provisions for 14 days. Some of the girls had secretly stored flour, butter, and eggs.

During the Easter week they got to work and baked. They managed to create 11 great *Striezel* [28]. We all stood at the table when they were brought in from the bakery, and we were so happy as only children can be. We had come together just like a family. I was at the head of it. None of the girls dared to do anything without first having asked me for my permission. We celebrated Easter Saturday almost as festively as we would do at home. All the girls were Catholic.

On Sunday morning, the entire group went to church for confession. In the meantime, I stayed at the post, made coffee, cut the cakes into slices, and set the table. When they came back, they found everything ready just as it would have been at home, and we enjoyed our meal together. We spent both holidays this way. Girls from other units came over and we acted as hosts. It was always my goal to make their lives as comfortable as possible because I knew that our time together was soon coming to an end and because it was so difficult to get enough food. The Easter celebration was, subconsciously, the conclusion of our being together.

On April 8, I was sent to Freimann [29] to get trained on combating tanks from a close distance. It might appear like a silly emotion if I had to describe how hard it was for the girls to see me leave. During the last days before my departure, they used every opportunity to do me favors. For me, this was proof of the correctness of my occupation as their commander. As relaxed as our coexistence was, none of the girls ever displayed any form of impertinence.

There is not much to report about the seminar. Soldiers from the various sections in the anti-aircraft gun units came together, but no one had the real wish to **(19)** achieve anything or to learn much from what was taught.

Following this period, events unfolded rapidly. After the return to my unit, I was promoted to head of the crew, which gave the girls in the unit some joy. On April 19, we received orders from Munich that our anti-aircraft searchlight unit was to be dissolved. *War Merit cross*

On April 20, First Lieutenant Dietz bestowed the KVK [30] 2nd class upon me. We both were cracking up about this ceremony. I wore it on my uniform only as long as I was still present in the commander's office, then I took it off and put it away into my wallet.

On April 21, I was transferred to unit 3/508 in Olching [31] to take over a post designed for anti-aircraft searchlight systems. That post was located in Schwabhausen between Dachau and Olching.

The following text appears under the heading:
"My Prisoner of War Camp Experience"

I want to divide it into: the final day in the post; the capture as prisoner of war; Heilbronn; Ludwigshafen; Stenay; and Metz.

I will try my best to describe the time as I actually experienced it, with no exaggeration, sober, and open, just as it is my way of doing it. Many things happened that cast a bad light on the Germans, when they are left among themselves. Many circumstances led to numerous disappointments felt by myself and my fellow soldiers with respect to our legitimate expectations towards the Americans. I will offer a characterization of the whole time which will be based on a comparison of how Germans treated Germans in 1933 and our treatment of prisoners in the Reich.

To begin with my explanations, I will first present the notes from my pocket calendar.

(20) April 28, 1945: I am sitting in my anti-aircraft gun unit awaiting the Americans. Everywhere around us you can hear the noise of the artillery and the tanks.

— POW

April 29, 1945: The Americans come marching into the village of Schwabhausen. We put down all weapons. Together with a corporal from the army, I left the post and surrendered as a prisoner of war. They take us in a car to Groß-Inzemoos. I sleep with many other soldiers there in the village's big farmer barn.

April 30, 1945: They take us by car to a remote village near Freising. In the evening, they take us to the military airport of Fürstenfeldbruck.

May 1, 1945: They take us by car from Fürstenfeldbruck to Heilbronn to a reception camp. We sleep there in the open without blankets, underpants, or tarpaulin. It is horribly cold. I got to know a fellow soldier with the name Conrad Schmidt from Fürth but lost sight of him the same day. In the camp there are 40,000 soldiers.

May 2: The first meal in the form of a light and a heavy can. No bread, little water. Very thirsty. The nights are a torture. Every day is rainy, at a minimum overcast and windy. Nowhere an option to warm up. With our pocket knives we cut the wooden light poles to get some

19

wood for a fire. Line up with other fellow soldiers in preparation for being taken to another camp. We are standing there from 7 p.m. in the evening until 4 a.m. March to the train station. Transport in open cars. It is raining during the ride. Nothing to eat. People on the outside throw some bread to us. We arrive in Mindenheim near Ludwigsburg in the evening. Again, no food. We camp in the open air, and it is still raining.

May 5, 1945: It is raining all day and partially also during the night. The first food in the form of one quarter of a liter of broth and one loaf of bread for five men.

Sunday, May 6, 1945: 11 a.m., we received half a liter of real coffee, later a piece of cheese, a cube of red beet, two spoons of soup. In the afternoon a ¼ liter of food. Weather is improving.

(21) May 7, 1945: The first blessing, the sun is shining. We feel a bit more cheerful, but there is the terrible hunger, hunger. They have established a kitchen in the camp in which are now 7,000 prisoners. To be able to wash and shave yourself is a luxury. There are pitiful scenes where they hand out water.

May 8, 1945: At 3 o'clock at night they hand out coffee; at 9 a.m. we receive some bread. At 1 p.m. we get a cup full of soup; many do collapse of hunger and because of the heat.

May 9, 1945: Every day there is much sunshine. We all suffer from thirst; there is now relatively good food, but not enough.

May 10, 1945: Much sunshine. There was a Protestant church service. A few Protestant ministers are among the prisoners and they are eager to win the souls of the disappointed fellow soldiers for eternal salvation. Our daily routine is always the same. Feeling hungry and waiting for what might come next. I expect that I will face several months of imprisonment. Yet, when I am thinking of the family, I feel very depressed. One must not allow your thoughts to wander off into that direction, but everything invites you to do just that: you sleep all day long and eat when anything is available. There is no intellectual or physical activity possible. The weather continues to be pleasant, but we are all afraid of imminent rain. Once that will happen, we will have no other option but to wander around day and night.

May 14, 1945: The first prisoners who are farmers are being released. They let 1,500 men go from the camp. Whether they are let go into life in civil society or sent off to a labor camp, we do not know.

May 15, 1945: There is a vaudeville performance, organized by some fellow soldiers.

May 20, 1945: Today was the day when the farmers were allegedly allowed to go home. The weather has been tolerable so far. The only drawback is the irregular food supply. One is so hungry that the knees become wobbly. I am firmly confident that it will not take very long until we will be released. Today, the first day of Pentecost, there was a great excitement in the ward. The cook sergeants, all of them Germans, had bartered away all kinds of provisions. This is a **(22)** sad sign how much the Germans make each other's life terrible when they are in misery.

May 23, 1945: Some of the prisoners are probably going to be released. We do not learn anything specific. One can be certain only about that which you see with your own eyes. My friend celebrated his birthday today. In the afternoon they placed me into another ward. Here I was questioned for the first time, but only scratching the surface. This move brought new suffering from hunger upon me.

May 25, 1945: I expect that I will be moved once again. Everyone believes that they will be released soon, but there is no clear

fear rain + cold

indication of that. I make every effort to hold out in patience. But I am afraid of one thing: the rainy season and the cold. It will certainly not be easy, when the weather will be cold and rainy during the day, to spend the night as well constantly walking. I would be happy if I had a tarpaulin or any blanket. Let us see what the situation will be like in the next camp.

→ On the evening of May 26, I felt quite depressed. One can clearly observe how much the condition in a full stomach determines the spiritual attitude.

On Sunday, May 27, at 7 a.m., they passed out coffee, which was hot and sweet. No one can imagine how invigorating such a real-bean coffee can be. The same day, move to yet another ward. It looks very likely that they will cheat us again with the food. It is and remains our impression that the Germans, who administer the individual prison wards, are nothing but thieves, whose most important task consists of stealing the food from their fellow soldiers.

On May 27, I was sent to another ward where a Russian was the administrator, and a Lithuanian the cook. Here, I encountered the best order regarding food and the distribution of meals.

May 28, again I have been sent to another ward. Everyone expects that we will be released, but, but...

(23) Today is Thursday, May 31, and we are still stuck in the ward. Compared to the other wards, our food supply is plenty and good. Nevertheless, we are still hungry. There is no indication that we might be released soon.

June 1, 1945. The new month immediately brings many changes right in the morning. 1,480 of us are loaded on to train cars, 40 in each. The ride takes us up along the left side of the Rhine, via Kaiserslautern, Neuenkirchen, Saarbrücken, Diedenhofen.

June 2, 1945, at 9 a.m., the train stops in Diedenhofen. The food supply has been very good, all in cans. Every man got 12 cans. But for how long? The afternoon has arrived. The whole day we were heading westward, so we got deeply into France. This means, we must adjust consequently and be prepared for a longer imprisonment. That is a bitter fact. In the afternoon we reached Stenay at 4 p.m., a little town between Verdun and Sedan.

taken to France

June 5, 1945: After various re-groupings we have finally reached our destination. The camp is situated in a French military barracks construction. Here is room for several thousands. Allegedly, this is a central camp from where the individual groups are supposed to be released. The rules in the camp are tolerable. The most important thing is that we are housed in tents. Every person got three blankets and cooking utensils. We are getting food two times a day. At 7 a.m. and at 5 p.m. They give us ½ liter of tasty coffee, but the food mostly consists of thin soup. On top of it 8 biscuits or bread. From time to time, we also get scrambled eggs or fish. The feeding of 1,500 men takes place within one hour. For all of us this represents a great relief. All the bickering and in-fighting is gone. The interactions among the comrades are more peaceful.

June 7, 1945: Today in the camp they took our personal data along with our fingerprints. There are, once again, new rumors as to our release and to the misdirection of our transport to the camp. **(24)** I am hungry the entire day.

June 8, 1945: We move into yet another ward. The effects of being imprisoned. Hunger, hunger, what will be the next?

June 9, 1945: The entire camp is doing forced labor. The reward for that is an additional liter of thin soup at noon. No one cares about the work. Everyone only wants to get the food. Because of the small portions of food, everyone has lost his strength. And then one is lying around all day. Once one gets up, one blacks out. I try to keep working with my remaining energy in order to maintain at least a modicum of energy.

Sunday, June 10, 1945: Today, work assignments again; food, as usual. Everyone is badly affected by hunger except for the kitchen personnel. There is hardly any conversation in which we would not talk about our hunger. In our most daring dreams, we wish for ourselves nothing but a dry piece of military bread.

June 11, 1945: I volunteered to work as a mason so that I can get the extra food.

June 12, 1945: On Monday we were actually supposed to be moved. So, we are just hanging out to be called upon. The philosophical analysis about where we will be going next started all over again.

June 15, 1945: We are loaded onto train cars in Stenay. Receive food for two days.

June 16, 1945: We arrive in Metz at 8 a.m. and are marched into a camp where we are supposed to do forced labor.

June 18, 1945: Today was the first time I worked. Found use of me as a blacksmith in a military auto repair shop. We still receive only little food. But there is hope for improvement.

Up to this point, these were the entries from my pocket calendar. Next follow the remarks from the attached pages.

April 29, 1945: We were taken prisoner in Niederroth near Dachau, from there transported to Groß-Inzemoos. The next day, Monday early morning, April 30, transported to Sern where we stayed in a barn. In the evening, transported to Fürstenfeldbruck.

May 1, 1945: Transported by car to Heilbronn.

May 5, 1945: Transported with a freight train from Heilbronn to Ludwigshafen on the Rhine, with no blankets or tarpaulins. The first days **(25)** we spend in the open air while it is raining. Very little food because there are too many people in the camp. Everything was arranged only provisionally; I established a friendship with a corporal from the army.

May 25, 1945: Time passes slowly. It has now been four weeks. Not an easy time. Hunger was and continues to be the worst of it all. We had good weather for two weeks, with lots of sunshine, meaning that we could recover from the cold during the previous days. Together with two other fellows we created a tent for ourselves. This helped us somewhat to withstand the cold without blankets. Life in imprisonment, under the given circumstances with hunger, thirst, and cold, exposes images of abasement of Germans no one would have thought believable, unless one would have witnessed them yourself. Only hope that those scenes will not end up in the propaganda movies of the victors. What I had predicted at the time when the Germans wallowed in victory has now come true. The German soldier in imprisonment, suffering from thirst, hunger, in part being poorly clothed, being exposed to the weather conditions, paints a poorer picture than the Russian living under even worse conditions. All such images presented to us in the weekly newsreels were completely tailored towards us. The only difference is that our food, though given to us in smaller portions, is of good quality and tasty.

Today, on May 27, we moved to a new camp that supposedly would bring us closer to our release. For a short period, we all suffered from terrible hunger, and this because those responsible for food in the other wards left us hanging out to dry. Once we adjusted to the ways the camp worked, food was relatively okay again.

May 28: We moved again. Probably the last stop on our trip. They will either release us into freedom, or send us to forced labor. Only for a short time, but still uncertain.

May 31: This uncertainty continues, alas. We are still stuck at the same place. The mood barometer of our souls rises and falls. It is a rather tough time for everyone who expects to be released into freedom, but nothing happens. **(26)** Everyone of the simpletons claims to have heard new shitty rumors. The result is that no one can stand the other because the tension among comrades is just too high.

June 2: The last days brought a decisive change. On June 1, we were loaded onto train cars together with sufficient food. The train moved into an unknown direction. Today we find ourselves deeper in France. Where will we end up when this is all over? It very much looks like it that this summer will be lost for us and our families. I hope this will be the last one. One must not allow the thoughts to turn toward home, otherwise deep anger rises up without one having a chance to direct it at those responsible for all this misery. For the future, there is nothing else to do but to grit your teeth and to keep hoping that our treatment, food provisions, and accommodations will be good. It is also necessary to take any opportunity for diversion in order to avoid losing one's mind.

June 3: Yesterday, we were unloaded from the train car in Stenay. It is a small town. The population treated us loyally. We were stationed on the open barrack yard. Everyone received a blanket. There was the rumor that the transport had taken us to the wrong place. Since we were all men whose professions were in transportation, traffic engineering, and agriculture, it would have been paradoxical to use us for work in France. Let us see what will happen. The key question is foremost how to fill our stomachs.

Today is July 23, and I have finished the transfer of the individual notes from my pocket calendar, and in the course of time I will write down my thoughts in the form as outlined at the beginning.

Metz, June 26, 1945

A quarter of a year in imprisonment. April 29 had also been a Sunday, like today. The day began with glorious sunshine. The American planes observing artillery movements flew over our post and the wider area. Once in a while you could hear a sheep.

(27) In the village Schwabhausen, the ⅞ [4] had turned toward fighting the enemy. On Saturday evening, three of us, corporal Koß, private first class Medinger, and myself had buried eighty bottles of Schnapps and a box with canned meat in the ground so that we could retrieve them later at a convenient time. The same evening, Koß had driven to Munich to take some of those delicious items to his wife. I never heard from him again. He could not return, as we later learned, because the Americans had already arrived and were everywhere. Private first class Medinger spent the whole morning in the village to make sure that our things were secure.

My box with the few possessions which I cherished I had already taken to the village in the morning. The Americans could come. No one was thinking of cooking food. We had taken our three-day meat provisions to the village so that the people could prepare it for dinner. It was my intention to leave the post in such a condition so everyone could see that we did not flee in panic. It would have been an easy thing for me to spend the mid-morning just in great debaucheries. Food items and drinks that we had missed for a long time were now available to us in great quantities.

But it was my principle, if I was to submit to imprisonment, then at least not intoxicated. As far as I could tell, I was prepared. Comrades from a telecommunication unit stationed in the village came and left, everyone with the strong feeling that something would happen soon. We discussed the way how imprisonment might happen. Nobody was even thinking of fighting. The telephone in our post rang from time to time, but we did not receive any significant orders or news, except for one order, once the enemy would have come close within a distance of 15 km, we should withdraw with all our gear to Obermenzing to our central combat headquarters. None of us were willing to follow this order because it was ridiculous from the start.

After I had gotten the post ready, as it seemed necessary to me, I wanted to calmly await everything coming my way. At 11 a.m., the head of the artillery unit said good-bye to all units via telephone. From my barrack I could overlook the state road connecting Munich with Augsburg.

(28) Suddenly the Americans arrived with their tanks, and infantry soldiers sitting on top of them. Then vehicle after vehicle rolled down the street which demonstrated to us the enemy's vast superiority in material resources. The tanks parked in front of us ready to fight. On Saturday evening, many of our troops had given up on taking the route through the village. Comparing these two different troop movements, the following verses fully apply to our case: "With a man and a horse and a cart, etc. ..." [32]

At noon, 4 comrades from the army arrived at our post, a corporal and 3 privates who had left their unit. They were exhausted and out of breath. As a first step, I provided them with food so that they could regain their strength. We allowed them to enjoy the real coffee, the Schnapps, and the meat from the cans. I even offered them cigarettes. Then we faced the question of what to do next. The natural thing was to make the weapons unusable and to put them away.

Then, a soldier came, who had stayed behind in the village and asked us who among us might be from Passau, and he actually found one. Equipped with an emergency package, they departed and tried to make their way to Passau. Others secured civilian clothes in the village in the belief that they would thus be able to get through without being detained. I took the position that once I will have to leave the post, it would be in uniform because I was a soldier. If the enemy wanted to apprehend me, then with or without uniform; for the administration and military posts, the only thing that mattered were the identity papers.

Before we all scattered, I made eggs that we kept in the post and distributed them to all the fellow soldiers. Then I also made pancakes. Everyone ate to fill one's stomach one more time. Then we prepared ourselves for the Walk to Canossa [33]. What should we take with us? One of us thought we should take our entire gear because he could not get it into his head that the war was over for us. Corporal Lehmann and I agreed that we ought to pack our bags with toiletry and shaving utensils, some underwear, and especially with food. I also took a military water bottle with me, though empty. In addition, I packed six cans of meat into a box and attached that with a hook to my belt. Thus equipped, we left the post.

We walked across the fields in the direction of **(29)** Groß-Inzemoos. Our goal was to reach that village where we could await the future development while staying with some of my acquaintances there. But we expected already all kinds of other possibilities. A large section of our hike took us through the forest. My new companion with the first name Walter had taken with him a bottle of champagne from the post. We emptied it during our hike. During our march we realized that the Americans had advanced farther than we had expected. Everywhere there were vehicles parked or driven around, and artillery batteries had been set up.

If we had any intention to avoid the enemy, it would have been easy for us because I knew the area well. But that was not our idea, so we marched straight ahead. At the first major road, we were stopped by a medical vehicle and told to walk toward an artillery platoon nearby. Now, we finally faced the ultimate imprisonment. I must also mention that, in case they might shoot at us, we carried a white flag with us, a towel attached to a stick. Once we had arrived at the platoon, we were immediately checked, then taken by car to the village Niederroth, from there to Groß-Inzemoos.

There, outside of the village inn on its meadow, was the collection point. A tragedy in miniature. In this village, where I felt like at home and where everyone knew me, I was a prisoner. My acquaintances stood outside, but I could not make any contact with them. Here again another personal search of our stuff. They took my pocket knife that I had kept with me since the earliest days of my military service and my nail files. When I checked the things, I noticed with horror that the box with the meat cans was gone.

After we had stood there on the meadow for hours, they took us to the barn of the party's village's farmers leader [21]. The number of prisoners had grown to 800. To get them all to lie down in the barn seemed just impossible. But it had to happen, with much cussing and cursing, like 'stupid dog' or 'pay attention' **(30)** and with much of the usual laments, screams, and complaints. I hardly slept that night. First, I was lying in a very uncomfortable position, and second, new prisoners arrived with great noisiness the whole night. One person screamed because he was lying underneath the hay, and someone had stepped on him. Another one searched for his clothing and could not find it. During the first days of imprisonment, we could already observe the signs of 'true' comradery.

On Monday, very early in the morning, we were taken out of the barn, loaded so tightly into cars that no one could move. Then we went off. One more last time, my gaze went over the anti-aircraft searchlight post and the entire well-known area, and then we moved into unknown territory. After a drive of ¾ of an hour we arrived at the country estate near Freising. There the same procedures took place as the day before. We had to stand there for hours. Each person's military unit was recorded. Then we were housed in a barn, which was then jammed-packed as well. Standing or sitting and almost reaching up to the highest beams, there were fellows from all military branches. Everyone was anxiously awaiting what came next.

Occasionally some of us were allowed to go outside to observe the call of nature. Right next to the gable wall they had dug a trench for that purpose. All the time, new prisoners were brought here by cars - officers and privates. All the new arrivals were driven to a meadow. The weather was April-like, partly sunshine, partly rain. But let us return to the first topic. We were glad to be in the barn and felt pity for our comrades placed on the meadow.

If we had had only a remote hunch of what was to come, our hearts might have skidded down our pants [34]. No one was even thinking of food for us. Most of us had a little food with us. But right from the start, hardly anyone had any bread. Both of us had precautionarily taken some military bread with us. Already then, we were forced to be harsh against ourselves and against others. For a slice of bread, they offered us cigarettes or meat, but we did not exchange anything, except in the case of some boys at the age of 15 to 17.

[handwritten margin notes: gave food to teenage soldier]

(31) Those boys had been used by the ᛋᛋ [4] for the defense of Dachau. At the crucial stage, the ᛋᛋ [4] had simply abandoned them to their own destiny, and they were helplessly stuck in their defense holes facing the American tanks until they were taken prisoners. So many of those boys lost their lives this way. They were brought to us, barely dressed, hungry, and frozen. They only owned cigarettes. They asked me for a slice of bread. I could not be such a barbarian to deny them their request. I gave one slice each to eight of them, with the result that there was hardly any bread left and as a result, not everyone got something to eat. My companion cussed at me for my generosity and made sinister prophecies about the future. The problem with water was the same. Since I was the lucky owner of a military water bottle, I was everyone's favorite.

[handwritten margin note: ran the camp]

Here in this barn, I got to know the fellow soldier Otto Schmidt from Fürth. We included him into our group of friends. By accident, I started a conversation with a man from the OT [35]. He wanted to reduce the weight of his gear and gave me a shirt and a 1-kilogram can with meat. We three then realized that we had to take great care, under the current circumstances, to consume our little food provisions sparingly and only within our small circle.

We spent the day standing, leaning against something, and lying down. In the evening, trucks arrived, the barn door opened and after we had been counted, we were loaded onto the vehicles. I had the great desire to be the first and thus to be transported away in the hope that at the next stage I would encounter better conditions. Then, the ride started. We were guarded by MP [36]. We drove through Dachau to Fürstenfeldbruck, and then we arrived at the military airport. Finally, everyone thought, we are getting a somewhat decent accommodation. But it did not go as quickly as we hoped. At first, there was the unavoidable long waiting. Then came the command: 'pick up gear and stand at attention.' Then we were counted for the umpteenth time, and only then were we allowed to enter the building, but not, as we assumed, to occupy the individual rooms, **(32)** but up to the highest level into the attic. There was no light; the floor consisted of cement and a thick layer of sand placed there to protect the building from aerial bombs. That was our new living quarters.

My two companions immediately laid down, irrespective of the possible danger of thereby risking to hurt their health. I spent the entire night standing, smoking one cigarette after the other. By itself a torture. But it was only a preparation for the nights to come. Here as well, new prisoners arrived constantly. I got repeatedly worried about how much weight the floor could bear. Everyone was squeezed next to each other, standing or lying down. The exit to get downstairs and to reach the well-known location [37], could be reached only with great difficulties, combined with a lot of cursing by the fellow prisoners who were disturbed in their position by this movement.

Each soldier was left with varying clothing and gear, all depending on what the Americans had taken away from them when they had taken them as prisoners, or depending on the circumstances of the capture. The manning of the anti-aircraft post Freimann, for instance, arrived with its full gear, ready for peace. Others, by contrast, owned nothing, not even a coat. Then again, there were those who had in their possession meat, bread, tobacco, and soap in large quantities. Thus, began a condition which many viewed as

prisoners stole for
ea. other

absolutely terrible and which has been accepted until today as a matter of fact. Everyone stole from the others, wherever possible. The fortunate owner of a backpack filled with all kinds of stuff today could be a poor man the next day, which was very common because there were some evil creatures who stole whatever they could.

Take this case, for instance: A corporal from my last unit, whom I had met in the attic in Fürstenfeldbruck, left to use the toilet. When he returned, his bag with cooking utensils, including a smoked sausage, was gone. But that night in Fürstenfeldbruck also passed.

(33) At 10 a.m., one MP [36] arrived and ordered those who had arrived first to prepare themselves for the transport to another camp, in which there would be better accommodations and what was even more important, better provisions. The existential fight began again. With pushing, shoving others, screaming and cussing, everyone tried to reach the narrow staircase from the attic, in order to get a spot on one of the trucks waiting for us. Our small support-each-other group [38] was one of the first and lucky ones. We succeeded to stay together, and as far as we were concerned, we were able to leave.

Finally, at noon, the caravan of about 20 trucks started to move. But where to?

We took the Reich highway, Munich – Augsburg. That was a stretch that was very familiar to me because I had used it during the last months several times with my bike going to Eurasburg. At Odelzhausen we left the Reich highway and continued using the state road. We went straight through Eurasburg, the place where I had worked previously. It was my secret hope that the trucks would stop in the middle of the village so that I could have an opportunity to contact the family Merkel. Even just for the simple reason to get some bread.

Dang it. Instead, we drove straight through this village with great speed. Someone looked out of a window at Merkel's, but I was not able to identify myself. So that was May 1st. It gave me an opportunity to compare today with previous May 1st days. The weather was cold and windy. No one knew our destination. We drove west and northwest. No one could move on the truck because we were packed like herrings. Only with great effort and a bothering of others could I reach my bag with bread. I do no longer know today which other towns we passed. Perhaps my memory will come back when I will have the possibility to reconstruct the drive on a map. At least **(34)** we went through a part of a beautiful German countryside which I would have liked to tour in times of peace as a free man.

We all were already quite starved. A few times, people managed to throw some food to us, but that was too little for an immense demand. The worst was that those without any conscience and the egoists grifted most of the food. The lowest instincts here prevailed without any limitations. Something else remains unforgettable for me. During the drive, the drivers took some breaks for them to eat. They had the well-known cans as provisions. In our condition, it caused us great effort to turn away our eyes from the good things. We were so outraged when the drivers threw the package with white sugar onto the street so that it burst open. They bit once or twice into the biscuit, then they threw it away. While we did not even know of such behavior during the best times of our lives, we felt that this was at that time a great sinfulness.

Now, after I have had repeated interactions with Americans at my current workplace, I know that the drivers did not think much about it, and did not have in the slightest way the intention to upset us. After all, this approach to food seems to be the American way of life, at least in the military. There is something else to report about the drive. I already mentioned that no one could move a bit. With the speed of the trucks, we experienced that in every curve the entire group turned to the corresponding side and those who stood at the platform gate of the truck had every reason to fear for their lives. Everyone cussed at everyone. In order to overcome this bad condition, we arranged for a warning system. From then on, every major curve was announced in time, and this had the result that through early changing of everyone's balance, the drive continued in this regard, without problems.

At one point I sang "The Hat Fell Off My Head but I Did Not Turn Around" as a low hanging tree branch had ripped off my cap. Now the wind totally ruffled my **(35)** hair so that I felt completely unrooted. It was really a condition to which one had to get used to. Preliminarily a knotted handkerchief served as a hat. At 10 p.m. we arrived in Heilbronn. A 10 hour drive on the bed of a truck, without food, without the possibility of using the bathroom. Now it was done, everyone thought. And expected the next things to come.

What we saw at first was not impressive. A town square, dimly lit, filled with MP [36]. Behind them a gate with guards on both sides, behind which our future was hiding. We could not see anything. We did not have time to ponder things extensively. Every group from a truck was counted, and ordered to pass the gate in a double-quick, under shouts of "lesko, lesko" [39]. (*lets go!*)

We stood in a square like helpless sheep, we did not know whether we should stay together or if we could do what we wanted. After a while, we dared to move. We barely could make out people. At every step that we took, it sounded as if the square were covered with skeletons. Our first question was, where is water, where are the accommodations? We were told there would be water provided only at certain times and then only after we had waited in lines for hours, perhaps. The accommodations would be there where we were, right there. As for food, we would have to wait till the next day.

Each day we would get a heavy and a light can. This explained to us what the reason for the clanging sound was when we walked. Some comrades warned us not to approach the barbed wire too closely because the soldiers would shoot at us. And that every day some of the prisoners had to pay for this carelessness with their health or even their life. Furthermore, we learned that up to now there were about 35,000 men in the camp. Now we knew everything that there was to know. Walter cussed, because of those facts, about our urging to get away from Fürstenfeldbruck. Otto simply sat down on his backpack in order to recover from the hardships **(36)** of the drive. We faced a long night. Walter was cold because he did not have a coat. I was cold because I had no underwear and only wore a miserable shirt.

Then Otto Schmidt gave me one of his underwear from the ones he owned. I put on this underwear and the shirt that I had received from the OT [35] man at night additionally to be better protected against the rigor of the weather. I will also never forget this night. I was deadly tired and exhausted from everything that had happened so far. In a rotation system we sat down and laid down on Otto's backpack. After a few minutes we had to get up because of the cold. While standing, our knees collapsed because we were so tired. Just like animals, we crawled together to hold and warm each other.

Starting with this night, the camping out in open air began. I am not a fanatic and I also do not develop hatred as a consequence. But there is one thing that I wished then and I still wish today, that every member of the Party [21] and every other enthusiastic supporter of the Nazis, would have to spend the weeks of imprisonment in open air conditions, which we as soldiers had to endure after several years of military service. At that moment, I certainly would have punched those in the faces without any hesitation who had been responsible for this.

The next morning, on May 2, I toured the camp in order to learn about the important things and to meet familiar faces. What I saw was depressing. Fellow prisoners did live either in tents or in foxholes as they formed small-group companionships equipped with just a few necessary things. Others walked around the entire night because they were lacking the basics. In some ways one felt taken back to the times of the first human beings on earth. In one of the holes, I met acquaintances. Lieutenant Schröder and several corporals from my previous unit. Then I took care of getting water for us.

Equipped with my own and Otto's military water bottles, I lined up for the water. Before that we had agreed in case, we lost each other out of sight to meet at a certain electric pole. To get water was a challenge by itself. Some **(37)** of the men tried to line up in a disciplined manner, even though this entailed hours of waiting, in order to arrange the dispensation of water without problems. In reality, it proved to be impossible because everyone believed he had suffered the longest and had the biggest thirst. Some of the higher-ranking officers believed to be, even in imprisonment, the chosen ones of Heaven, and walked without consideration of the many who lined up, directly to the source. That triggered loud shouting every time, and no one felt obliged to observe the order that we had established with great efforts. I stood there for 3 hours, maintaining my self-discipline.

When I eventually reached the faucet, I noticed with horror that it had dried up. Full of disappointment, I left, but the thirst was even stronger. During the long wait for water, all the prisoners in the camp were told through loudspeakers to prepare themselves to receive food. For this purpose, the mass of people was ordered to move to a piece of land in the back. The number of prisoners had grown to over 40,000. It will be understandable for everyone what it means to direct so many people who are resting on a square without any formal association into a certain direction. The best comparison for this would be a large herd of sheep. I did not find my 2 fellow soldiers at the arranged spot. So, I joined the stream of people, always looking out for my two fellows. By itself, an impossible thing to do.

The handing out of food happened as follows: After the front part of the square had been cleared of people and the mass had been shaped into various columns, every individual had to march by the stapled boxes containing the food and received 2 cans in a rushed manner. Then one was allowed to stay only on the cleared square which would thus avoid anyone from receiving a second handout. The preparation for this handout took about 7 hours, eating just five minutes. With truly voracious hunger, everyone devoured the little bit of food. Only the well-offs, because of their fuller stomachs, were able to manage the valuable food content of the cans thriftily.

I met Walter at the prearranged (38) meeting point. Otto was and remained lost. We had eaten, and no one was really full. What mattered then was to prepare for the imminent night. With an empty can, we dug a hole. Walter had found a tarpaulin. During the handing out of food, I had taken an empty cardboard box with me, which served as a base for the bottom. It was a sacred object. I could not dare to put it down, otherwise it would have been taken away from me immediately. There was no water on that day. I took a little gulp from Walter's military water bottle. That night we spent in a hole that we had dug within a bomb crater. We sat very close to each other and on top of us was the tarpaulin. We were tired enough and yet the cold weather in the morning awoke us from the deep sleep. We opened our eyes and stood up. Thus, we were ready for the new day. No way to wash oneself. By stretching the body, the worst dirt had fallen off. We had little trouble with food. A part of Walter's military bread was still there and 3 cans of meat.

One slice of bread for each of us and we shared one can of meat. That was our breakfast. When will we get our next food, that was the question. After we held our 'council of war' we decided to create a better sleeping area. We asked a comrade to join us, who also owned a tarpaulin, and with that, we built a roof. The rest of the morning, I tried to obtain water but without success. Then, the usual preparations started for the handing out of food. We carried all of our possessions with us at all times because nothing was secure. People offered cigarettes for a small piece of wood to build a tent or to cook. The possibility to secure water became even more difficult. Some fellow prisoners offered 20 cigarettes for a gulp of water. After we had received our food, I lined up again and again for water. To describe the conditions in detail is impossible. You would have to experience it yourself. I did not get any water. Almost half crazy because of thirst, I staggered to our earth hole. Then finally they handed out water from a truck in pitchers.

Here, I had **(39)** success for the first time and got a drinking cup filled with water. Somebody announced via the loudspeaker that 3,000 men could line up at the gate to be transported to yet another camp. We three abandoned our not-yet-proven companionship and lined up. That was 7 p.m. Instead of the requested 3,000 men, about 10,000 pushed forward.

Our position was favorable. We were pretty much up front. My thirst was so great that I walked from here to the nearby water place. Disregarding the camp police and the military police guard, I pushed my way to the faucet and drank and drank. Like an animal, I poured the liquid that I had missed for such a long time into me. Then, I filled the cooking utensil and both of my military water bottles, and I was saved. After I had returned to my place, Walter did the same. During the lining up, I experienced the first mean act by a fellow prisoner. After I had shared the water in my cooking utensil to those standing around me, a fellow prisoner asked me to lend him the cooking utensil. In order not to appear selfish I gave it to him.

I never saw the cooking utensil or the fellow again. A disappointment which I could not overcome for a long time. At this position we stood till 4 a.m. That means, for some time we stood, then we leaned back-to-back, then we sat down or squatted down. Always a new position. We could never stand any one of those for long. This night was also a torture.

Finally, it seemed to get going. There was a lot of cursing, screaming, or even begging, while we were counted out of this mass of people, always a hundred. Those had to interlock their arms to keep together. And the way we were pushed in we were pushed out again. We who had been at the head of them all at first, had been pushed rudely far backwards. But, nevertheless, we managed it. Once again, we had achieved something. In the front square the

39

authorities split us into marching block formations, marching units, who were guided by the military police to the train station.

(40) Here a 'luxurious' train, which consisted of a long row of open and covered cars, awaited us. The loading took place quickly. I no longer remember how many men were in each car. At any rate, so many that no one could fall. Now we were in the cars, and as far as we were concerned, we were ready to move on. But the Americans did not care about us. It took a long time before the train finally moved. In the car, there was the usual situation. At first a lot of screaming for a spot, but then we had to accept the reality that we had to cope with the very limited space. My military water bottle, or rather its content, was very much desired by others. People offered me many cigarettes for a cup of water.

Already at the beginning of the train ride, the fellow prisoners would have drunk all the water. In this case, however, I remained absolutely resolute. I was in an open coal car. The train started to move with the pace of a Swabian railroad train [40]. It is not my strength to remember all the train stations. We drove through Heidelberg, then near Mannheim we crossed the river Rhine on an emergency bridge, through Ludwigshafen to Mindenheim.

During the ride, the military guards shot with their guns in the air to shoo the civil population away from the train. For sensitive people, this ride was perfect to soften up or, at least, to think about this parody of life: to ride through Germany as a prisoner, the acts of craziness of the last weeks of the war constantly in front of our eyes, that is, in the form of senseless destruction of bridges and villages. From the windows in the houses, women and children waved at us. Many women cried. The way we looked was cause enough for that, considering that we had not washed or shaved for six days. Plus, hollow-eyed because of hunger. When we talked to people, we learned that many such trains had come through. Everywhere they threw food and tobacco for us to catch.

But to the shame of the German prisoners, I must admit that those things were rarely shared as good companions would do.

Whoever stood at the window or the board wall, took those things and kept them for himself, **(41)** or they were cliques who looked out only for their own interest without any consideration whether there were fellow prisoners standing right next to them who barely could keep standing because they were so hungry. In one case, I observed that, on the next day in the new camp, one soldier still ate from the same loaf of bread that had been tossed by people. Considered carefully, this was an obvious case of cheating of the fellow comrades in the car. In the afternoon, the train stopped in the open landscape, in the vicinity of a village. "Everyone out!" We had to get out of the car, stand in military formation, count, and march. We could see the camp from the train. March into the camp.

At the gate, military police with batons, but they used those mostly only to swing them demonstratively. I cannot testify about any direct torture or mistreatment by the guards. In general, we had hardly any contact with Americans, and if so, only when we switched to another prisoner-of-war camp. Almost all organization activities were overseen by German camp police. That is one of the sad chapters to which I will have to return later.

In the camp, we were placed in an open square. Here, they divided us in groups by nationality and ethnicity: Hungarians, Austrians, Poles, Bohemian Germans, etc. were sorted out. We used every opportunity to get water and to use the toilets. Those were in the middle of the square. It was completely absurd to think of private spaces. To release ourselves was of course no longer the action of merely physical needs. The conditions of imprisonment had the consequences of some suffering from diarrhea which was almost like Typhus, others suffered from constipation.

For what it is worth.

Line up, count, count, attention, whatever, we were obtuse to all of that. Finally, the order came: march. We marched on a long country road. Single numbered wards occupied with prisoners who were in the same condition as we were. Buckets with food were carried back and forth, and we gazed after them with desire. A gate protected with barbed wire opened up: in a long row we marched into the camp. **(42)** What we found was a free piece of land, covered with low growing wheat. No barracks, no tents. A guard from the anti-aircraft unit, who later turned out to be the leader of the camp, assigned us a parcel of land where we had to stay. Nothing to eat for today. We first assessed the situation and then secured a little piece of terrain as our housing for ourselves. Clever fellow prisoners immediately went to work to tear out the half-grown wheat to use it as a base for the night.

We both ate some of our provisions, but it was only a small meal. Walter shared his pessimistic observations about our efforts to get away from Heilbronn. We were badly disappointed in our belief that we would get to a better camp. We had no other choice but to prepare our sleeping area for the night in Granada [41]. On the first night, it began to rain. On top of the cold, there was now the moisture. Our only protection was the tarpaulin which offered, of course, not enough protection for two men. I would have liked to take off the boots that I had worn since the first day of the imprisonment. But I could not dare to do that because I would not have been able to put them on again.

On the other hand, this condition triggered a strong disruption of my blood circulation which made it impossible for me to go to sleep. Early in the morning the rain forced us to get up. We had not had any rest, of course. Hungry, tired, and frozen we stumbled through the camp. As a protection against the rain, I had put on a canvas jacket covering my head. Slowly but surely the rain penetrated every piece of clothing, down to the skin. The ground was soaked, and with every step you had to watch out that the boots did not get stuck in the mud. Nevertheless, we had to march so that this movement kept us a little warm. We were so tired that we caught ourselves repeatedly falling asleep while standing with our knees buckling. Some of the fellow prisoners were lying flat in the mud despite the miserable weather because they lacked the strength to keep standing.

Under these circumstances we were increasingly reminded of the question of how to fill our stomachs. A rumor slowly spread that we were supposed to get something to eat. The only problem was that it was complicated because **(43)** the meals had to be transported from the main kitchen. The kitchen for the camp itself was still in the process of being built. Those were good perspectives which did not allow us to develop much optimism. I had some difficulties with Walter in this regard because he was, by nature, a pessimist. During the mid-morning, it got a little better.

Finally, we got the long-awaited command: "Group 12 receive your food!" One of our group's master sergeants was appointed as the authorized person to manage the organizational and food commercial matters for our group.

September 1, 1945

I have not written for a couple of weeks. Not that I did not have enough time, but I lacked the motivation. Sometimes I even reflected, if only I had not started with this diary. The entire time of the imprisonment is a constant up and down in our physical and spiritual condition. An important factor for all this is the quality and quantity of the provisions and the way of our living together. The impressions from the challenging past weeks fade away in that process.

I will try to connect with my last lines.

We got our first warm meal in Ludwigshafen. Everyone got a drinking cup full of food. Hundreds of pairs of eyes followed every movement of the handing out of food so that no one ever got a little more than the others. Lucky was the one who owned an empty can in which he could fill the food. Hardly any of the prisoners had ever scraped their eating utensils so thoroughly in their previous life as we did then scrape our cans. If you could no longer get anything with your spoon, then the pointer finger did the rest. All characteristics of a good civic education were unscrupulously thrown overboard. After all, hunger hurts. This lasted for six weeks. Every food handed-out was quite an ordeal. Orders were yelled, people screamed, they bickered and hit each other regularly. No one got enough. No one can imagine what problems emerged, **(44)** when there was leftover food. To share this little bit equally was not an easy task. Sometimes it was handled as follows.

The group of 100 men was subdivided into 10 smaller groups, each with a leader. Those leaders received an equal share of the left-overs and passed it out spoon by spoon among their 10 men. The same happened with coffee and tea, only with the difference that the coffee grounds were also passed out because we ate it out of hunger. Once each group got a box full of biscuits, 60 in total. Thus, each person got ¾ of a biscuit. Cheese and sugar always had to be divided up into 100 parts. Everyone thought to embody justice as long as one got the largest piece. We got bread in various quantities. Sometimes 10 men got one loaf, sometimes 5 men got one loaf. Recently, 4 men had to share one loaf. Water was always a problem. It happened repeatedly that hundreds lined up for hours and then did not get anything after all because the kitchen staff had priority. At the same time the weather was so hot that the people collapsed like flies.

Under those circumstances I witnessed that the camp leader, a German master sergeant from the anti-aircraft unit, brutally hit people in their faces with his fist because they could no longer observe discipline out of the torture of thirst and because of the long wait. Most people lined up at night because they did not have a place to stay or could not go to sleep due to the cold.

To maintain order in the camps, the Americans had selected officers from among the prisoners, who used their authority similar to the ⚡⚡ [4] by getting batons without asking for permission with which they could demonstrate their authority. This camp police earned an 'everlasting reputation'. The same was the case with the kitchen staff. As I had mentioned already on one of the previous pages, all kitchen administrations that were occupied by Germans bartered away the food and cheated the fellow prisoners in a shitty way.

I will return to the reason for this later.

(45) Obviously, such circumstances had an impact on people's health. First, the great disappointment about the way this imprisonment was handled for all of us. Then, everyone hoped day by day for a release. The reason for that was that the American leader of the camp had promulgated something to that effect on the first day of Pentecost. Most of us were not even clear about the political and military collapse of our country. Many believed, and continue to believe, that it would be a reasonable expectation that the countries that won the war would treat us humanely and decently just because we are Germans. There are still many among our ranks with the opinion that we had treated our prisoners in a better way [42].

Diarrhea, almost like Typhus, was common among almost all of us. Many ran to the latrines and yet did not arrive in a condition as he had hoped. The cleaning up was not easy, especially if you consider that often there was not even a can with water. This allows me now to turn to the chapter 'cleanliness'. During the first six days washing was a luxury. Also shaving. Thanks to our ingeniousness in turning the nights to days, we always were lucky owners of a small supply of water. The 1-kilogram can was the vessel for washing, drinking, and eating. There were also plenty of lice. What else could we have wished for? At any time of the day, one could meet people who were devotedly dedicated to the hunt for lice. Under those circumstances, no one gained a victory, despite the highest number of killings.

Earlier, I used the term 'latrine.' This word needs commenting. How often have we applied or heard the term 'perfume of the latrine,' without thinking much about its meaning. Here in the prisoner-of-war camp one quickly understood its true meaning. While 'giving birth' that could take hours or happen rather quickly, people debated world politics quite strategically, without getting any more clarity about the true reason for our misery. In most cases, Hitler was regarded as the man who had wanted to do the right thing, but the others [unfinished thought].

(46) The Nazi propaganda had had such good success that some already predicted the war Russia versus America and wanted, for that reason, to volunteer with the Americans. Everything that was voiced here through the mouth should really have been emitted immediately from the behind but circulated later as the latest news throughout the camp. One told it to another, assuring him that he had heard it from a reliable source. Endless conversations and discussions erupted during which people got rather heated. Everyone believed in, hoped for, doubted, and hoped again for something, and at the end he had to realize that it was all trash. If there were no other topics, then people talked about food. If there was someone who brutally and openly stated his opinion about the situation based on his political understanding, he was called a jerk, traitor of the fatherland, or friend of the Americans.

Only food gave us some diversion, which was handed out to us at outrageous times, and then also the registration of each of our professions. Here one could notice that many claimed the one profession that seemed to be most fitting - at that moment - for a person to be released from imprisonment. Such a condition ruled in all camps, Heilbronn, Ludwigshafen, Stenay. There was only one small difference that began in Metz.

Metz, September 22, 1945

Many weeks have passed, since I have written the previous lines. Today as well, it is hard for me to write about the time in Metz.

But why? Well, because I am filled, the clothing is good, and the accommodations as well. The working conditions are manageable. Yet, I still want to capture the key aspects from that time.

On June 16, we arrived in Metz. Marching on foot, we crossed the city and reached a camp in the yard of a factory at the end of the city. Our column of men looked miserable. Hollow-eyed, we were hungry and especially pessimistic. In the new camp we were at first called up by our names. **(47)** Then, they announced to us that we would be grouped as work units. The organizational structure was the same as in the German military. There was a leader of the unit, a constable, and a secretary. A Lieutenant Colonel commanded several units. For all of us, it was actually a disappointment to be once again under the command of German officers. In the aftermath we did not pay any attention to them, at least not more than was necessary, and regarded them as an unavoidable nuisance. No one observed the required rule of saluting them.

As for our accommodation, we got a factory building that had been badly damaged by bombs. The roof had holes, and there were no glass panes in the windows. The best thing was that this accommodation had stone walls and a floor of concrete. We faced a daunting task to fix the damages. During the first two days, we were fed as in Ludwigshafen. Without any transition, things continued in a new way. They selected staff personnel for the kitchen from our ranks. It was interesting to observe that almost everyone claimed to have been a cook or that one had at least once fetched coal for a kitchen. All this out of the desire to be as close as possible to the source.

On Monday, June 18, the work began. They took us with trucks to the workplace. This was located in Metz. After we had been registered and divvied up again, we were assigned our jobs. We were assigned to a garage-company for an American car repair shop. My assignment was as a blacksmith and welder. From then on, the days passed homogeneously. At 8 a.m. we were driven to the seminar.

At 11:30 a.m. we returned. At 1 p.m. we left again, and back at 5 p.m. Apart from a few weeks in July during which we worked after dinner until 10 p.m., nothing changed the entire time. The food was good and yet, it was never to be enough. The reason was that the previous period **(48)** had emaciated us too much. We got then, and still get, three meals per day. In the morning, bread, biscuits with or without jam, or scrambled eggs. Noon: vegetable soup, red beets, or pudding. In the evening: milk soup and bread or biscuits and coffee. The menu and especially the amount of food always depended on the quantity that the kitchen had received as appropriation. The slightest amount of more or less in food was commented on with the corresponding appreciation. When it was more than usual, everyone was all smiles, but when it was less, then the kitchen staff had to face sharp criticism although they generally could not help it.

Our behavior was actually quite understandable. Our physical weakness became twice as much noticeable while working. In the morning or at noon, when we had to wait for the trucks, we were not able to stand for a longer period of time. We sat cross-legged like the Japanese, spending the time waiting. Almost all conversations ended in fighting because all were, despite the food that had been handed out before, still hungry and disgruntled. Those weeks were probably the hardest for us, apart from the one in Ludwigshafen and Stenay, in imprisonment. During the work our limbs trembled, and when we had to bend down and then stretched again, we faced a near black-out. The treatment by the Americans at our workplace and the entire collaboration was decent and benevolent. I am glad that I did not write about this time during those hard weeks because I now notice, while I am fully fed and content, that one needs to be in such a condition in order to comment objectively about those things.

(49) Christmas 1945

The time just flew by. Eight months in imprisonment. Many of us believed that we would be home for Christmas, but unfortunately... The fact that this is not the case is not the worst. Worse is that the majority of us do not have any possibility to get in written contact with their families. That is bitter. Even though the imprisonment is not so hard on me, I still would very much like my family to be informed about me, so that they would not have to worry about my destiny. Life here is monotonous. Two times per day we leave the camp, and two times we return to the camp, and dang, the day is gone. In the evening we sit around the table and talk stupid stuff, and off to bed. So, it is day by day. This condition is interrupted only occasionally when we have a free day.

January 1, 1946

The old year has passed. It has brought us a lot. Less pleasant things were amongst it. The new year begins. What will it bring? The PWs [43] at least, expect to be released to freedom. As far as I can judge the situation, I expect this to happen in the first half of the new year. Nevertheless, it is possible that I might be wrong in my assumption. The officials have not indicated anything regarding the matter of a release.

The fellow prisoners wish each other good luck for the new year and associate all kinds of hopeful thinking with it. This is all shady business anyway. I do not wish anyone anything for the new year. Yet, I must accept good wishes and must return them if I do not want to be impolite. Ruthlessly, I put aside all my inner mood and feelings. Hold up your head, look straight forward, do not let anyone get you to lose your hope for the socialist future. That is the way how I will enter the new year.

(50) January 1, 1946

Dear Wife!

A new year begins. Once again, my thoughts wander backwards. The last new year celebration I had enjoyed in an anti-aircraft unit near Augsburg together with eleven girls. It was nice only if one ignores everything else.

Already at that time, my worries for you and the children depressed me. For eight weeks, I have not received any mail. What might have happened at home? Every day I asked at the post office whether there was a letter for me, but nothing. Also, when I had come back to Dachau, no mail.

Completely as a surprise, I received furlough. How happy I was. On a Sunday morning, I drove, facing a wild snowstorm, to Dachau to the central command post to get my furlough papers. From there, I started my trip, without having anything to eat during the train ride. Anton Kölbl, whom I met on the train, quickly shared with me a slice of bread and a piece of sausage.

The train ride was as it was expected considering the war, coming along with all the typical harassment, delays, overcrowding, and windows with holes on the train. During the train ride, there was an alarm about a possible aircraft attack. Nevertheless, I arrived home on Monday morning. No one among you had the slightest idea. But how quickly did those days pass. To say good-bye was very hard for all of us. The first time during my military service you accompanied me to the train station. We knew that many worrisome things were awaiting us. It did not take long for them to arrive.

The difficulties with the mail service grew considerably, and soon no letters arrived any longer. On the second Easter Sunday, I received your last letter. It did not contain good news: bomb attacks, hunger, Kurt [44] had been killed in the war, etc. On that day I had it. Particularly during the Easter holiday, I had plenty to eat, and yet I knew that you at home suffered from hunger which was bad. It spoiled my appetite. But by means of my usual approach to all things in life, I managed to get all of this behind me. The military events were tumbling. The fronts were shifting at a fast pace to our disadvantage.

(51) Then came the capture. Finally, the time has come, I thought, and so many others. This time did also not end without disappointment. Now eight months have passed. No mail contact, no news from home. I do not know whether you have survived the collapse. Constantly my thoughts wander off. What will they do? What will happen with Herbert? Does he still go to school, or did he have to take up a job? Do the children even live? Is the apartment still in good shape, and so many other things? No answer for any of these questions. There is no way for me to get discouraged.

I firmly believe that you and the children are still alive. Furthermore, I also believe that the authorities of the new time do provide help, as far as the conditions permit. Dear Wife, keep up your courage and do not despair, even if life seems to be so hard. One day, I shall be released. Then, I will be able to take on the responsibilities for you and the children again. And thus, to relieve you of a major part of your bundle of worries. In the hope that these small expectations will come true, I am starting the new year. I wish for you and the children health and the strength to sustain the harshness of life with a smiling face. When that will be possible for you, then everything will be well again. Greetings to you and the children,

Your husband.

(52) – Page 52 is blank.

(53) Here is an article, which I had sent in the middle of September [45] to the newspaper that was being produced in the camp, which was also published.

Between Despair and Hope

No question is as important to the prisoner of war as the one pertaining to the release. But when one must listen every day to the various speculations about that, one feels compelled to express some fundamental thoughts.

The little news in the newspaper or radio concerning this question that reach us are not useful in any way in drawing positive conclusions, because one news contradicts another, or they overlap each other. Why, we do not know. All other announcements which emerge over and over again in the form of latrine rumors, such as "release to the French" or "we will never be released," and so many others, are particularly not useful in creating clarity about this circumstance. On the contrary, they only cause confusion and have the effect that the mood barometer of the fellow prisoners, depending on one's nature and on the quality of the rumor, rises or falls. The interest in such question is understandable, but it has damaging effects when it happens as outlined above. In order to find the right attitude, perhaps the following lines might be helpful.

We lost the war. In the past, the defeated part had to always pay the price. And this is the case with us as well. To what extent the individual carries guilt must be addressed somewhere else. With the end of the war, it becomes particularly difficult for us, as prisoners of war, as we do not have, for the time being, a fatherland with an independent government. And that the control of our destiny is entrusted to the effective thinking and actions of the responsible leaders of the victorious states. Some authoritative voices have repeatedly said that these countries have absolutely no interest in making the German people pay for it more than the circumstances **(54)** require. Such statements and the consideration of economic and ethical principles of life must be motivation for each of us to maintain a firm faith and hope.

Let us get to the essence of it.

The military and political collapse with all its accompanying circumstances was so horrible for both the German people and us as soldiers that the majority of people stopped believing in anything. If we are to continue with such an attitude, life would not be worth living. This cannot be.

Hence, we need to trust and believe in the future, neither blindly nor fanatically, but following a complete reversal of our thinking, deliberate and consciously by scrutinizing ambiguity. If we all could do that while still in captivity, we will do a lot for our people. Because it is not about the one or the other individual or, even more reprehensibly, just about the ME, it is about the long-standing imperative to form a society, about all of us, and about us as the people and our continued existence as a people.

Our release, once having become a reality, sooner or later, is the beginning for new tasks and a new life. Everyone must firmly believe that, outside in the larger community, there is a place for everyone when one has a clear political goal before one's eyes.

Metz, September 10, 1945

(55) – Page 55 is blank.

(56) – Page 56 is blank.

(57) April 1, 1946

Once again, a free day. Month passes after month. The days run by uniformly. Spring has arrived. Dawn arrives earlier, and daylight stays on until later in the evening. For us prisoners this works to our advantage in that we can spend the evening hours outside. Here in the camp, we do everything we can to make the building inside as comfortable as possible. Every free corner is transformed into a useful setting. Resting benches and flower pots are placed, and whatever is necessary. If all those things by themselves would make up the meaning of all of life, we should actually feel like in paradise.

How do I spend a free day? Above all, I sleep longer in the morning. It is nice to be able to stay in bed when the others must leave for work. After the troop of workers has left, I get up, go to the washroom, and do the morning cleaning. Afterwards, I drink coffee. I give this activity my full attention and with joy. Then, I clean the corner of the hall where I live. Well, then I face the question of what to do next. Either I secure a book for myself and read, or I write on these pages.

I have asked myself quite often whether it is useful or makes sense to write, and I have reached the conclusion to keep doing it irrespective of purpose and meaningfulness, just because I find a diversion that is fitting for me. No one bothers me in this activity, and I do not have to participate in empty conversations. Somehow, I actually manage to capture the conditions of the imprisonment, which later might be interesting for me, or at least for my children. There are many things that make me think, especially the new political formation of Germany.

This aspect is the greatest mental burden for me, to be far away and to only watch from a distance. When one observes the criminal play of those forces, invisible to those who do not understand anything of politics, how they want to construct a

Germany politically without any strength and in that process utilize, as it seems, self-proclaimed authoritative circles, one could almost give way to despair. Hitler had often enough claimed that he had **(58)** learned from history, so that a second 1918 [46] would not repeat itself. At the time, people smirked at it, provided that they had already become aware of the megalomania of this man.

It is a crime, of its own kind, when social democratic leaders today, whose politics during the 15 years of the Weimar Republic had led to fascism and to 12 years of evil terror that brought Germany to the brink of an economic collapse, try to undermine the strong impulse to possibly pull the exsanguinated and exhausted people [47] out of its misery by a broad coalition of antifascists. What under Hitler as megalomania and craving for political recognition or the committed crimes was paired with intelligence, does not apply to these people. We ought to expect and demand from true Socialists a better understanding of the current necessary political goals and decisions. What however motivates these people to act as they do? Incompetence or cowardice.

It is no surprise, when one hears and reads the news, that many people in Germany reach the conclusion that they were better off with the Nazis. Here, we face once again the beginnings like it was when we had many parties [48], when the Nazis fattened themselves from the mistakes committed by the SPD [49]. One thing I have realized here during imprisonment for a long time is that the vast majority of the German people are absolutely not receptive and, in part, not worth to be governed with democratic measures. As far as one can learn from the printed media about the process of the denazification in various regions, the same happens here in imprisonment.

Releases, as far as they are granted, are not practiced according to any political criteria. Thus, it can happen that some are released who had been party members [21], whereas others, who had suffered in the Third Reich and served time in a concentration camp or prison, are required to stay here. It requires a pretty energetic effort to oppose, in our small circles, the glorification of national-socialist ideals. How else could it be possible that fellow prisoners, when they learn from some excerpts of the Nuremberg Trial, formulate their enthusiasm about the grandiose posture by Hermann Göring. **(59)** These are the conditions of imprisonment. When I encounter such things, I resolutely share my opinion.

But enough of that. I wanted to write about the sequence of a free day. Hence, I am writing. There is so much I could write about. But sometimes it does not flow. In general, the day is interrupted only by meals. In the afternoon one takes a shower, and in the evening the fellow prisoners return. We are six men at one table and eat our meal together. Until the time to go to sleep, we gather in groups and may have either pleasant or uncomfortable conversations.

The conversation becomes a bit more pleasant when people tell obscene jokes, or when we tease each other and expose each other's weaknesses and failures. It becomes immediately unpleasant when anyone by accident mentions political or ethical problems. There are only few with whom you can discuss seriously and objectively fundamental questions, without turning into a fight. I must add that the German, despite his alleged political education, is politically stupid because of the twelve years of National Socialism. People who held ranks militarily or in private life, suddenly turn out, when dealing with the simplest political questions, to be children.

To describe in more detail the sequence of my days does not seem to be worthwhile. Maybe I will do it when the imprisonment will last for me for too long. I have taken on a new task for me: to summarize my time in the military. In my case, the situation is that, for me, nothing in life is meaningless.

My Time in the Military

As it was for me as for many Germans, I would never have thought of becoming a soldier. Not, perhaps, because I would not have thought myself physically fit enough. No, it was the structure of the state. Before 1933, there was the professional army, the Reichswehr. At that time, only those who were particularly physically fit were accepted. In 1929, I suddenly had the idea of joining the Reichswehr. I however distanced myself from it when a police corporal of the relevant police ward advised me, **(60)** when I applied for a certificate of conduct that I change my political position. In the red youth-front, a sub-group of the KPD [50], I acquired basic military training. It helped me later during the few weeks that I spent in a concentration camp.

That was the end of that until, with the arrival of the new period, things suddenly changed. In 1937 or 1938, I was drafted. Replacement Reserve #I was the tactical term for my level of serviceability in the military. In August 1939, I received the first draft order to show up at my unit. My employer, however, got a release for me as U.K. [51]. For me, this did not mean at all a relief.

The work conditions constantly became worse because a huge number of well-trained men were also drafted, and the employment agency did not send us any corresponding replacements. One more time, I was able to avoid being drafted because of a new U.K. [51]. The third time, when I got a draft order, it was over. No one in the firm could help me avoid it any longer. I personally did not care. Such a destiny that had become reality already for millions, I could no longer escape.

On August 1, 1941, I had to report to the 43rd anti-aircraft unit in Wittenberg on the river Elbe. The reception there was as usual as endless waiting, then names were noted down, read out loud, and then again waiting, until we were finally assigned to rooms and organized by squads, platoons, and companies. I was assigned to a machinist unit with the purpose of being trained to operate the anti-aircraft searchlight unit equipment. The entire platoon was an anti-aircraft battery. The entire training ran its usual course. It was divided into infantry basics, practical and theoretical equipment operation, and general instructions. We had to practice and learn all those things *ad nauseam*.

At the beginning of October, the training was complete. According to the announcements of the authority figures, we were supposed to be sent to the front. But where to? No one knew. One day we started. With complete gear we went to the train station. The train took off in the direction of northern Germany. The final station was Aalhorn in Oldenburg. From there they took us to an airforce base. Here was the official regiment headquarter, which took control of us and assigned us to the various units. Together with 75 men, I came to a unit that had just started to be formed. The fellow soldiers who had sighed with relief when the gate of the barracks had closed behind them, were mightily disappointed. There, the entire group **(61)** was brutally trained once again for seven weeks. We experienced our *Blaues Wunder* [52]. The chief of the platoon was an ambitious representative of the German Barrass grinding machine industry [53]. I passed this time well, since as a well-trained athlete serving in the infantry, it did not get to me.

On November 7, 1941, we moved into our post. And that is, from Lingen in the Emsland, where we were stationed across the surrounding area. According to military nomenclature, we were now on the front. The individual units consisted of 10 to 16 men. Our task was to serve the airforce at night. At that time, they had set up a belt of searchlight units from Schleswig-Holstein to the coast of France, with the purpose of making the enemy planes visible for our airplane pilots when they tried to fly over our territory, by means of shining light on them. The entire time we spent was about keeping guard, exercising, and practicing for alarms. I cannot say anything about capturing even one airplane by means of our searchlight efforts during that time. At that post, I was promoted to vice searchlight officer.

In May 1942, the charge to chase enemy airplanes at night was suddenly abandoned. Our unit was transferred to Munich. My first post was near Munich in Laufzorn, near Deisenhofen. My function was, as before, machinist. At the beginning we hardly faced any attacks. As result, our superiors went crazier and crazier. In August

1942, I was ordered to attend a 14-day VR [54] seminar. Our platoon chief wanted to make me a radio eavesdropper under any circumstances, but I absolutely did not want to become one. From that time on, there began my migrations through the various posts. Always just for a few weeks of service:

Römerschanze, Stuttgart, Deisenhofen, Großdingharting, Troß, Deisenhofen, Taufkirchen, Oedenpullach, Geiselgasteig, Deisenhofen. From here, I was sent, in May 1943, to an U.A. [55] re-examination course in the vicinity of Starnberg. In the last six locations, I served as an anti-aircraft corporal. The chief told me repeatedly that he wanted to send me to a staff sergeant re-examination course, but he did not do it. I was curious whether it ever would become reality.

As a noteworthy incident, I must mention the execution of a corporal, **(62)** who had been condemned to death, which took place in March 1943 and at which I was ordered to take part. That was the first and last time that I participated in the execution of a human as it was a military order.

After various changes of posts, I was sent to Augsburg on January 8, 1944 for another staff sergeant training. It lasted until February 18. During that time, I had been transferred away from my unit and landed after various odysseys at the 1/508 unit in Gilding-Argeloried. I did not stay here for long. In this platoon, I was promoted to corporal, and after a short period, I was transferred to the 4/508 unit to Dachau.

In this platoon, I assumed the searchlight unit post in Groß-Inzemoos, where I stayed until October 10, 1944. From then on, I was in charge of training women in Friedrichshafen until December 10. Subsequently, we set up a platoon of women in Eurasburg near Friedberg. In this platoon, I had the function of the leader of the communication unit. In January, I returned to the old platoon in Groß-Inzemoos. Here also a unit with women. In April, a course about fighting tanks in close proximity. Then, still various changes to diverse posts. On April 22, I had to leave that platoon and had to move to the 3/508 unit located in Olching. Here, I was positioned in Schwabhausen and in this location, I concluded my military service as it ended with the capture by the Americans on April 29, 1945.

(63) Metz, January 21, 1946

I am a prisoner housed in a factory hall, together with more than a hundred fellow comrades. On both sides of the hall, beds are arranged on three levels, as we were used to them from the days during our military service. Always two and two structures placed together. This then establishes a so-called living community. In front of this bed structure is a table with two benches. From the table, one can look to the right and to the left throughout the hall. The fellow prisoners sit around, alone or in groups, after they have returned from their work assignments, and they sit at the table busy with reading or with having conversations. This still life is interrupted only by the meals. Above all of that there is radio music, the one bridge that mentally connects us with the world.

What kind of conversations do people have? Topic number one, in this case, is the question of a release. This is a topic which is always acute and inexhaustible. People ponder, back and forth, possibilities and constellations. One who has never been a prisoner does not know anything about such conditions and would probably never understand or grasp it. I know this condition already from the time when I was imprisoned for a few weeks in a concentration camp. At that time, a fellow told me that he needed to get out of there at any cost. He was not at all willing to accept such a long time of uncertainty and hence, he was willing to betray everything, including himself. Another one said, he would rather spend several years in prison or do hard labor knowing that he will be released on such and such day, than facing an indeterminate time in a concentration camp.

And that is the way it is here.

During conversations about getting released, one can hear fellow prisoners talk pessimistically and with little hope. There are only a few who oppose such pessimism with a healthy portion of optimism. It is, of course, difficult to preach hope, good advice and faith, because everyone has been disappointed several times during the long months of imprisonment. In these matters, it would be appropriate to possess the running-amok faith of a religious fanatic. At least one ought to be clear that **(64)** one is both a soldier and a man, and therefore one does not have the right to become weak and lose hope. Even though the circumstances are as dire as they are. Most regard their personal fate as the hardest thing in their life, without considering what misery the war has brought to the home country.

What is it that we really do suffer? Nothing!

There is enough food to eat. The same with tobacco. Clothing clean and good. Without difficulties one is able to replace the ripped pieces of clothes. Accommodation and bed. We do not need to worry about heating. Of course, there is barbed wire around all of this.

Herein rests a contrary perspective which cannot be offset against materialistic calculations. The barbed wire is the symbol for the separation from home. It limits our personal freedom. It limits us in our ability to act and to plan. When thoughts want to take off for us to sort out the future, then suddenly there is the barbed wire, and one stops, full of resignation. Some fellow prisoners have already compared it with a golden cage. One has all material things which the body needs, and yet one suffers greatly. These circumstances are certainly hard to bear this misery.

Let us look at the flip side. Through the news from the press, radio, and from letters, we know that our families struggle materially very much. Little to eat, in many cases miserable accommodations, difficulties with provisioning and upkeep of clothing, almost no heating, and on top of it, a spiritual suffering of not knowing about the destiny of their father, son, or brother. They are not surrounded by barbed wire but by worse elements, such as military occupation, political and ethnic division, intrigues, envy, and discord, economic hardship, moral endangerment and ruins. Wherever you look, ruins. Whose situation is therefore worse?

(65) Sunday, February 10, 1946

For the first time in a long period, it is a Sunday that I am spending in the camp. Most of the time I go to the workplace. On labor-free days one easily gets tempted to reflect upon one's destiny, and then one is not far away from getting a moral hangover. Patience, patience, and even more patience is required to get through this time. Every day, we discuss amongst ourselves the question of our release. If one loses self-discipline, another one cries like a little child. The simplest things that make life worth living are taken away from us. How much would I like to hold a child's hand or to stroke a child. How much would I like sometimes to just chat with a woman.

These are all things that we were bereft more or less of during the long time of military service. How often does one ask oneself, how is the family doing? Have they survived the time, are all the children still well? Currently, I do not imagine that anything bad might have happened. I simply trust that everything is well. Many fellow prisoners have received mail from home. One day, I will receive some as well.

Based on everything that one learns from newspapers and radio, one can assume that it might be even quite good that we are still imprisoned. The economic and food conditions seem to be in such a way that it will certainly take a long time to bring back home all the prisoners of war and to reintegrate them into society.

One could simply rationalize such incomprehensible conditions, as they have affected major parts of humankind, by recognizing the criminal actions by the former fascist leaders of the state as the cause for it. One could also regard it as one milestone in the fight of humankind and in its search for justice and truth, brought upon us by cosmic forces whose laws we cannot understand, and therefore not comprehend.

This situation looks very differently, when you regard the things from **(66)** a political viewpoint. Someone who, like me, has been active in political life since I was 13, can well dare to entertain reflections of such kind.

I gained the first political impressions during the time of the collapse of 1918.

My parents descended from well situated middle-class conditions and were traditionally German nationalists. This type of thinking was foundational for my education. I attended grade school for eight years. I was taught religion. The political changes of 1918 confronted us as students with a need to voice a personal opinion about religion as a matter of education. We had to decide either between religion or social studies. My parents allowed me to decide on my own and I opted for religion. That was also the time of the great workers' strikes. Among them, there was the strike of the miners in the mining district of Zwickau, Lugau [56], and Oelsnitz [57].

They demanded decent wages. Those demands were never completely met to the full satisfaction of the strikers. In most cases, the actions were ousted by means of state forces. In my last school year, I distributed the Communist newspaper *Der Kämpfer* [58]. I never lacked any newspaper readings. My parents at that time subscribed to four newspapers, of which each represented the orientation of one of the larger parties. That provided me with the opportunity, in connection with observations about real life, to form my own and firm opinion. My two brothers, whose profession was masonry, had found their way to the Communist party via trade unions. A major event of a political kind at that time was the invasion of Saxony by the *Reichswehr* [59], with the goal to restore peace and order, allegedly endangered under the red Fleissner government [60]. After I had left school on Easter 1924, my confirmation was all but the last ritual in church.

Around that time, one of my brothers was thrown in prison for the first time because he had illegally distributed forbidden Communist newspapers. All compelling reasons for me to assess the political and economic structure of the state, to **(67)** understand the reasons for such passion for politics and what paths individual parties promulgate that they believed would be best to overcome all mischief.

After the collapse of 1918, the former imperial German Reich had transformed into a Republic [61]. Its representative elements were a Reich president, at that time Fritz Ebert [62], a Reich parliament, and the various state parliaments. The rights and privileges of each German were anchored in the Weimar constitution. Everyone was supposed to have the right to voice a free opinion. The strongest and leading party was the Social Democratic Party of Germany. Well-known representatives of this party sanctioned, in their function as representatives of the state, their signature of the Treaty of Versailles.

Once the Treaty of Versailles was sealed, the economic impoverishment of the German people was contractually determined for years to come. This condition made it possible for the reactionary forces at the same time, by raising the deceptive question, who had been responsible for the war, to win over dissatisfied nationalistic sections of the people for their ideas.

The goal of those circles was to organize a new movement, which intended to restore an old-world German dominance. In order to gain influence among the broad masses, this movement put on a deceptive cloak by way of formulating social and revolutionary demands, a movement that was supported by high-power finance forces.

The Social Democratic Party, governing the country and being supported by the broad mass of workers and by a portion of the bourgeoisie, had assumed the task, to guarantee the fulfillment of the Versailles Treaty. They engaged with all their affiliated organizations for this purpose. One of the most important one among them were the free German trade unions. One of the central mottos of the SPD

[49] was: 'vote for us, and through our majority in the parliament we will develop socialism.' They rejected the approach pursued by the Russian people in order to realize their own destiny, exactly like both the fascist and the royalist **(68)** parties. Because of this stance by the SPD [49] the class conscious and revolutionary forces had split from this party and merged via the USPD [63] with the Communist Party.

The Communist Party differed fundamentally from the other parties in its goals, and until today it does so. It realized that the working class, as the guarantee for the existence of a nation, was ruled without rights and power. The education of the working class lies in the hands of the ruling class as the property-owning class. Hence, humanity is divided into the class of those who are exploited and the class of the exploiters. The latter, a miniscule group, rule by means of owning the large-scale industry, the land, and by controlling the money, and, using tradition and in part driven by greed for profit, have assumed possession during the last decades. This class claims to represent the nation. By means of its influence this class also controls the entire religious, cultural, political, and public life.

In order to realize its political and economic goals, it does not care about the interests of the broad masses. Without any mercy, those circles let millions of people starve and to bleed to death, and to die in misery. That was the way it looked until 1933. On one hand, mass poverty, visible in the form of the large number of unemployed. On the other hand, merciless greed for profit, also characterized by the number of unemployed. The mass of workers, farmers, and small craftsmen were looking for an escape.

The development had demonstrated that a solution was not possible by means of the permitted democratic measures. The people had voted more than enough and became more and more disappointed going from one election to the next. What mattered then was to decide on a party that contained in its program fundamental changes. The parties that offered such changes were the KPD [50] and the NSDAP [21]. The NSDAP [21] opposed the

Communist Party that wanted to change the form of government, as a joint movement of the workers and the middle class, **(69)** by means of a non-parliamentary revolutionary fight.

The NSDAP [21] instead aimed to gain an overwhelming majority in the parliament and then to replace the democratic structure with the dictatorship with Hitler as the leader. This party, which combined the terms 'national' and 'social' in its name, had cut away many votes from the SPD [49] that aimed for compromise and accommodation and as a result, soon enjoyed the largest number of members [64]. The intention of this Nazi party [21] was not only to free Germany from this economic misery, but to establish Germany, by using the economic misery, as a stronghold against the Soviet Union and against Communism, shielding it from large democracies.

In every assembly, during every public march, in every newspaper the KPD [50] admonished and warned: "Protect the Soviet Union," "Hitler means war," "He who votes for Hitler votes for war." Those were the slogans with which the KPD [50] pointed out the dangers of fascism. The German people, or at least the people who had committed to this national socialism, were deaf to these warnings. The Social Democratic Party, whose leadership might have been able, by way of a radical change of its own course, to confront this danger, failed, either out of weakness or, what is more likely, because it was already so strongly associated with the capitalist state so that it regarded Communism as the greater evil and rather preferred to deliver itself to the gallows.

In the year 1932, when Severing, then the Prussian Minister of the Interior, was removed from his office through the efforts on the right, the KPD [50] appealed to the mass of the SPD [49] to immediately respond with united protest strikes and protest manifestations so that the fascists would understand that the working class paid attention.

That appeal did not go anywhere. The leadership of the SPD [49] continued to just watch passively the gradual preparations of the fascists to take over power. The number of class-conscious workers and functionaries of the KPD [50] who were apprehended and thrown into jails and prisons grew exponentially. In parallel, bans on media assemblies and **(70)** public marches were issued. The crowning of all was when the terror elections were held on March 6, 1933.

Up to that time, the fascists did everything to avoid open provocations by means of extra-parliamentary general actions, such as the organized fight against the class-conscious forces among the KPD [50] and SPD [49]. That was also the time during which the majority of people embraced the opinion, "just let Hitler take reign for once. If he does not achieve anything, he will just have to leave." During the year 1933, many still assumed that he would not be able to hold on to power for more than a year.

The greatest actions of the KPD [50], during the last months and before Hitler's seizing of power, consisted of organizing the Antifascist Unified Front. There were protest marches when Hitler assumed the post of the Reich chancellor on January 30. The last effort was the protest march of the anti-fascist front in February or in April. Here in Zwickau, we had larger demonstrations than ever existed in the workers' movement. By then, however, it was too late to avert the danger because many believed that participating in this march was enough to fight against fascism. Skillfully, at the time, the authorities in charge of public order avoided intervening in any provocative manner, and the entire protest march happened peacefully. Large portions of the workers had become aware for the first time how much power rests in the unification of the masses.

(71) Metz, May 18, 1946

Today I am forced to write something about the camp. Here, we have a camp newspaper that gets published weekly and has the purpose, apart from providing general entertainment, to inform about the current events in the world. Officers were in charge of it. The editors changed several times. The fundamental tone of the newspaper was in no way democratic. At least one or the other editor tried, via translations of relevant articles in American newspapers, to prepare us for the changed conditions which we would encounter at some point.

During the last weeks, the editor changed once again. And under the management of the new guy, the newspaper radically assumed a provocative tone. I saw myself obligated to voice my opinion with the following article.

Reflections about and for the Camp Newspaper

People come. People go. This is the way in the land and so it is also in our camp with camp-spies. There have been already some who have tried by means of using the camp newspaper to have an 'inseminating' impact on us.

As far as I know, the newspaper has the purpose to inform people about events in the world, so that they can gain a broader picture and based on it, can perhaps also formulate an opinion. In the past, everything essential had been masterminded for us and was presented in a corresponding format in the newspaper or the radio. One only had to nod approvingly and thus to annex those products as one's own opinion. Opposing them was not to one's advantage.

Our camp newspaper serves about 1,200 men, who generally depend, apart from the radio news to which they listen only half-heartedly, on the content of the camp newspaper. Times have changed. Probably many have not noticed it or have not understood it.

It would be the least one could expect from a newspaper that it contributed to making the incomprehensible **(72)** comprehensible. When I read the last camp newspaper, I concluded it is a "tabloid paper". The editor hides busily behind articles from "Stars and Stripes" in a form that people, whose inclinations is to correspond to these kinds of articles, experience a personal internal parade and probably reach the conclusion that we were, and still are, great guys. Perhaps some realize more strongly that we actually, only through an unfortunate accident, are stuck unjustly in imprisonment.

One is almost tempted to shout out "Hosiannah" [65] about the nature of the common German but we stop breathing because for some of the most important question: potatoes with or without peels? I really have to say, I was deeply moved by this call for aesthetics coming from the circles of PWs [43]. First, because my boy at home told me in the first letter that I had received last week that they had eaten the last potato at Christmas in the form of potato soup. And yet, my wife is at home with seven children. On the other hand, I was moved how skillfully an internal matter in the camp has been brought to the awareness of our caretakers.

The German Character has Proved Itself

In a large internment camp, I have experienced that a similar question had been brilliantly resolved with a beating stick. We ought to be glad that our caretakers do not judge things of that kind with German objectivity, otherwise it would have long been brought to our knowledge where the most and best vitamins rest in a potato.

The result from all of this is "Splinter and Beam." [66]

Take a good look at yourself in the mirror [67] to intensively steer even more attention to yourself and then, examine the environment next to you. If a newspaper at all, then one with a common-sense undertone. Even if many readers accept this kind of reporting without expressing their own position, I will not stay quiet. Expected attacks and strikes are welcome to share with me.

Häber, 5th Company

(73) This article appeared in the newspaper, but it was cut down, changed and supplemented with a response by the editorial team

in such a form that did not address the core of the matter and instead attacked me personally. My fellow prisoners advised me to beat up the responsible person. I did not do that. I confronted the idiot by reproaching him for the meanness of his action and alerted him that he would get an answer to the article so that all members of the camp would be made aware of it.

The next evening, I placed the following note on the bulletin board of all 6 companies:

Since the editorial team of the camp newspaper is not able to publish the article of a "Democrat" in the way it was written, but has systematically falsified the meaning in part and the structure of the article, I am forced to make my position known this way. The editorial team probably assumes that the intellectual level of the prisoners in the camp is lower than their own, and hence makes an effort to translate, throughout the article, 'foreign words', although those are generally understandable. With respect to solving problems in an American collection camp using a club, it was not the American camp authority, but the German camp police.

Concerning potatoes, they have probably thought to lecture the kitchen staff with the article. Despite it all, the confidence in the objectivity of the newspaper "Between Home and Barbed Wire" has increased. The answer to my article in the camp newspaper began with this sentence: "The first Democrat has voiced his opinion."

(74) – Page 74 is blank.

(75) – Page 75 as it appears in original diary at this point of the writing showing the Russian alphabet and a Russian vocabulary.

(76) – Page 76 as it appears in original diary at this point of the writing showing the Russian alphabet and a Russian vocabulary.

PYCCKHH алфавнт

a , b , w , g , d , je , sche , S , i , K , Л , L , m , n
Aa, Gb, В, Г, Д, Ee, Ж, З, И, К, ,Л, М, Н

o , p , r , ss , t , u , f , ch , z , tsch , sch , schtsch , ä , ju
О, Л, р, С, Т, У, Ф, Х, Ц, Ч, Ш, Щ , З, Ю,

ja, jo, i ü j, Hartzeichen, Weichzeichen,
Я, е, Ы, ъ bI

ГОВОРИТЬ = sprechen   Я = ich = ja
goworith
                          Ты = du = Ti

ОН = er = on

ОНа = sie = ona

ОНО = es = ono

Мы = wir = müi

ОНИ = sie = oni   3.Person Mehrzahl

          ГОВОРИТЬ:
Я = ich = ja   ГОВОР/Ю = spreche = gowor/ju

Ты = du = Ti   ГОВОР/ЕШ = sprichst = gowor/jesch

ОН, ОНа, ОНО,   ГОВОР/ЕТ = spricht = gowor/jett
er, sie, es,   sprechen
on, ona, ono,   spricht

Мы = wir = müi,   ГОВОР/ЕМ = sprechen = gowor/jem

76

ВЫ - ihr - wüi   ГОВОР/ете = sprecht = gowor/jettje

ОНИ = sie - oni   ГОВОР/ЯТ - sprechen - goworjatt

ХОТеТЬ = wollen - chottjett

Я = ich - ja   ХОТ/Ю - will - chott/ju = ГОВОР/Ю sprechen = gowor/jatt

ТЫ = du = Ti   ХОТ/еш - willst - chottfjesch   ГОВОРИТЬ = sprechen

ОН = er - on   ХОТ/еТ - will = chott/jett   ГОВОРИТЬ - '

МЫ = wir - mui ХОТ/ЮМ - wollen = chottjum   ГОВОРИТЬ - '

ВЫ = ihr - wüi ХОТ/еТе - wollt - chottjettje ГОВОРИТЬ - '

НеТ = net - nein ,   ЄЛЯ = dla - für

ЄЯ - Ta - ja   С = - mit

КЯК = kak - wie   У = - bei, an

ГЄе = tje = wo   Я = ja, ТЫ = du, ОН = er, ЫЛ = bill Vergangenheit

КУЄЯ = Kuta = wohin

ЯТКУЯ = atkuta = woher   Я = ja, ТЫ = du, ОНЯ = sie, ЫЛЯ = billa weiblich

ПО = po = auf, über   МЫ = wir, ВЫ = ihr, ОНИ = sie, ЫЛИ = billi Mehrzahl

К = K = zugegen

В - w = in, noch

(77) May 30, 1946

Today it is Ascension Day. On May 21, I was moved, together with 60 other fellow prisoners, to another camp in Metz. The unit to which I had been assigned was dissolved. There are many indications that the end of the imprisonment is in sight. One assignment after the other is coming to an end. Nevertheless, no one expects too much. At one point, they surely will have to release us. One must not stick too much to specific dates, otherwise one will not get out of the loop of disappointments. I notice for myself that life in imprisonment leaves traces. For months, I have been waiting for mail. Always in vain. So far only one letter from Herbert has reached me that informed me that they are all still alive. But how does this weigh against the hunger for news from home? In the old camp, I left behind many good fellow prisoners.

In August of last year, during my work assignment, I had designed and built a barbell, hoping to begin with sports again. But the flesh was weak, as willing as my spirit was. For a long time, the barbell was lying around and was used only by the athletic kitchen guys. Everyone laughed at me and thought that I was crazy because I wanted to begin with sports at a time when most of them did not move more than necessary because of their hunger. For a long time, I ignored the barbell. One day, I got the idea to build a wrestling mat. I found some fellows who thought like me. After we had secured the tarp, wood shavings, and a sewing kit, we started the project one evening. Five men were involved in this.

Over the period of eight evenings, the mat was done. We had started lifting weights already before that. In the meantime, November had arrived, and the room in which we trained was pretty cold. But we did not let this bother us. Once we had finished the mat, we organized regular times for exercises in the evenings. The first evening began. There were not many active athletes among us but all the more spectators. Courageously we threw ourselves into it. The result was that all of those who participated ended up, more or less, with pulled muscles and sprains. I got injured quite badly too, which caused terrible pain that lasted for several months. It was obvious that we could not expose our bodies that were fed with just milk soup to the physical stress as we were used to in the past.

(78) Hence, we ended up with only one evening. The cold and early darkness, and all other things typical of winter, did not allow for any regular exercises. Only when Spring arrived, some showed interest again. For me, it was more difficult because I was assigned to a work group that labored for twelve hours a day. But one day, some fellow prisoners approached me and told me that athletes from another camp wanted to compete against us in wrestling. From then on, I began to reorganize the whole thing. At my workplace, I built another barbell at which we could increase the weight systematically. Then I scheduled two training evenings per week. Now, this time the efforts resulted in real success.

In a short period of time, I had assembled a group of 25-30 active athletes. We lifted weights, we wrestled, and did also light track sports. For the entire group in the camp, I also built a high bar, a set of gymnastic rings and ropes for climbing, and a pommel horse. All this equipment was intensively used.

I was then very suddenly pulled out of these activities because I was transferred to my current camp. I do not believe that it is worth starting all those things here once again. During the 14 days which I have spent here so far in this camp, I have never left my room, except for getting food and going to work. There are 12 men per room. All people have come from different camps. We spend our free time reading. Repeatedly, I tried writing, but felt horribly about it. Our conversations are always the same: mostly silly conversations. As soon as we start serious talks, people show a variety of opinions. At the end, all talking ends with the topic of when we will be released.

Sometimes, I think that this writing is nonsense and yet, it is still my most favorite activity because it forces me to steer my thoughts into a specific direction. The main thing is that I will be able to take these pages with me when I will be released, so that I will not have to talk too much. Then, my wife and children can take this little booklet and choose for themselves what interests them. I hope it will not last that much longer, so that one can be a human being again among human beings and must no longer deal with such a monotonous life.

(79) My Workplaces - June 3, 1946

On Easter 1924, I graduated from school. Apprenticeship from 1924 to the Fall of 1927 as a blacksmith for shoeing horses and building carts with Willy Mittenzweig in Culitzsch near Wilkau [68]. For 14 days I worked for a small-scale smithy in Niederalbertsdorf near Werdau. I stopped with this work because I made too little money and then there was no work overall. I went to Roßlau to my sister to find a job there. I stayed there for 3 days, then I went to Berlin to see Kurt. I walked through Berlin for 8 days without finding work. I went back to Zwickau. I arrived there on a Saturday evening. The next Tuesday, I began working for master blacksmith Otto Richter. I worked there for a year.

From there I switched to Arthur Wittig in Zwickau. I worked there for one day. I injured myself with a blue thumb and took sick-leave, only to quit altogether because that place was nothing but trash. 14 days I spent in Langenhessen near Werdau. I quit that job because it was too lonely in the countryside. I found a new workplace with Hans König in Zwickau. I worked for him from October to January. I was then laid off because there was not enough work. I was unemployed for 14 days. The next 14 days I worked in the Maximilian mine as an ironworker.

I was let go again because there was no work due to the strike in an auxiliary factory. I was unemployed for a short time. Then I was hired by the city to work as a snow remover, until the middle of March. I was let go and began the next day as a blacksmith in the repair shop of the Reich train repair factory. On October 19, 1929, I was let go because there was not enough work. I immediately began to work for my original master with whom I had apprenticed and worked there until January 1930. From then on unemployed until 1933. During that time of unemployment, I worked unofficially for the coal dealer Otto Geipel.

From May 1933 to May 1934, I spent time in pre-trial detention. From May 1934 to June 1935, I worked as a coachman for the farmer Arno Schmidt in Lichtentanne near Zwickau. Thereafter, I worked as an assembly helper for the firm Thyssen-Dresden in the construction of a factory building for the Auto Union [69] until July. Then, I was a roof tile carrier for a construction firm from Doberlug/Niederlausitz assisting in the building of a roof. I was let go when the project was done. For three weeks, I worked as an assistant for a roofer on Richard Street. I was let go because there was no more work. Until December 5, I worked as a temporary worker for a governmental project to regulate the river Mulde by a firm from Chrimmitschau in Crossen. There, I quit on my own and started as an occasional worker for the mover firm Neundorff in Zwickau. I worked there until I was drafted by the military.

(80) My Time as an Apprentice

What do you want to learn? I faced that question before I graduated from school. Otto and Kurt had become masons; hence, I wanted to become a carpenter. Before the last year of school, a scholarship gave me the opportunity to attend high school, but I rejected it because I did not see myself fit for suffering from hunger resulting from studying. As it was common for my age, many jobs seemed attractive. In fact, it took a long time until I found an apprenticeship. Easter was just around the corner. One day, I read an ad in the newspaper in which a blacksmith apprentice was offered. Until that time, I actually did not have any relationship with this kind of craftsmanship, except that my grandfather had been a blacksmith.

At any rate, I urged my father to respond to this ad in writing. He did not really care what I wanted to learn, so he sent a letter. Then, we waited for a response.

One evening, when I came back home from playing, I was asked: "Where have you been"? The blacksmith from Culitzsch was here. I was so curious. The following Sunday, I wanted to go there with my father so that they could check me out. Sunday came when my father and I left home. Culitzsch is located about 15 km distant from Zwickau.

We took the streetcar to Wilkau, and from there we walked, towards Kirchberg, always along the narrow-gauge train track. My future master owned an inn, a smithy, and a farm. Our negotiations were quickly settled. They looked at me to see if I would be strong enough physically to meet the work requirements. They agreed that I would stay there and would receive room and board. The salary was 50 *Pfennige* [70] per week during the first year. After my father had finished several glasses of beer, we returned home. My master wanted to pick me up on the third Easter holiday with a horse-drawn carriage. No one can imagine how proud I was, first, because I had an apprenticeship, and second, as a blacksmith.

I made myself a black apron using a piece of leather that Hulda [71] had sent from Brazil. I also got a pair of wooden clogs. I could not wait to begin with the work. I also got to own a large suitcase that Hulda [71] had also sent. I stowed everything that I had to take with me into it. **(81)** One could have almost assumed that this was for a transatlantic voyage.

Finally, the time had come. One afternoon my master arrived with a light coach wagon and with a large brown mare. The farewell was brief and painless, since my new place was not beyond the world. I felt like a king. I did not speak much with my master during the trip. Soon we had left the city behind us. While we drove through Wilkau, I witnessed that my master was known everywhere. Everywhere I heard "Good luck, Will." When we arrived, the children, a boy and a girl of 8 and 11 years old, appeared and stared at me.

The wife of the master showed me my room, and I carried my suitcase upstairs. It was right under the roof.

At the gable was a window, and where I was resting my head in the bed, there was a round window in the size of a full moon. From there, I could look onto the street and watch narrow-gauge railway trains drive by. Once I had provisionally accommodated myself in my room, I went downstairs to eat. Afterwards, the children showed me the smithy and the garden and everything else that seemed worth being shown. The house next door was also owned by my master. In that house lived five families with many children. This now was my new sphere of activities.

The next day life became serious. At 6 o'clock, I was woken up and we immediately went to the smithy. The first thing I had to learn was how to make a fire. This work created much trouble for me during the first few weeks. When I believed that the wood had started to burn and started to pull the bellows, the fire went out again. When it took too long, I was reprimanded. Eventually the work began. Hitting on the iron with a big hammer. When the master said "hit it" then that meant for me to take the hammer and to strike. Quite often I missed. I was happy for every strike that hit properly. Whenever I missed, I received good scolding so much that my hair stood on end.

(82) My master was a short man [72]. As short as he was, as loud and long could he curse. Endless swearing with all possible ornamentation he could utter. On the first day, I hurt my pointing finger of my right hand so much that it turned blue. That was a great beginning and, at the same time, a warning to quickly overcome my clumsiness. The finger hurt so badly that in the evening I could not stand the pain. Until that time, I had not said anything. Now I was crying. My finger was at first appropriately admired, and then they pulled a thread through the big blister so that the blood could be drained to relieve the pain. Thus, one day passed after another. Food was good.

As in every aspect of life, so here as well, step by step, I acquired the practical knowledge of the craft. During the first few days, my master once said to me, when I had been very clumsy once again, "Just tell me, kid, what have you ever done at home." At one time, after shoeing a horse, I had to take it to the Schröter mill in Wilkau. "Hold it close to the halter, then nothing can happen." With great fear I started on my trip. More and more I let out the rope because I was afraid the horse would step on me. On top of all the unfortunate circumstances, the narrow-gauge railway train from Wilkau passed by. The horse, normally quite harmless, but now a little emboldened because of the loose rope, whinnied and jogged at the end of the rope. Horrified, I took it to a lamp post, wrapped the rope several times around it and thus waited until the train had passed. When it was all over and I had returned the horse to the stables, without it having been hurt, I breathed a sigh of relief.

Later I have often laughed about this. After all there was no greater joy for me to bring a horse to its owners especially when it was a little bit lively. Mostly I used the bike for this purpose, sat on the bike, and then a wild chase broke loose. I enjoyed good friendships with the boys in the neighborhood. They were Heinz, Erich, and Kurt, as well as the Roigers boys. They kept calling me **(83)** "the blacksmith apprentice." The children often teased me by singing this rhyme: "Blacksmith, blacksmith, take the little hammer with you, when you want to shoe a horse you must carry the little hammer, you certainly do." When this got too wild, I grabbed one of them and taught him a lesson.

The work schedule was not firmly determined. I was woken up at 6 a.m. I jumped out of bed, put on the pants, placed the blue frock under my arm and rushed downstairs. The first assignment was to feed the horses. Then I started the fire in the smithy. During this time, the master also appeared, and so the work began. Every morning we forged eight horse shoes. I gave it all with my body and soul. Near the fire, I stood behind the master and pulled the bellows until the iron was red-hot. We barely exchanged words. The master only said the little phrase, "hit it," and I jumped over to the anvil.

The master took the red-hot iron out of the fire, cooled down the heat with sprinkles of water, and the forging began. First, he had to form the shoe's thigh, then he folded it and punched the holes. Half of the shoe was done. Thus, we continued until all eight shoes were done in a raw form. For my ears, there was no other beautiful music than the rhythmic interplay of both of our hammers. Beginning with the ringing signal of the hand-hammer held by the master onto the black anvil, and then the first hit by the sledgehammer that I held in my hand. Thereupon began the hewing of the metal piece.

First the hit by the hand-hammer, then shortly thereafter the hit with my sledgehammer directly onto the anvil, as a sign that the workpiece was expanded. A short well-aimed hit with the hand-hammer meant the end of the work with this piece. This was the way we worked every morning. If I ever really overslept, I was then certainly woken up because the master then played a symphony on the anvil, which woke up the entire neighborhood. After that he mostly called up to me: "Are you not soon getting up; I guess you are waiting until the sun is shining into your eyes."

As soon as this work was finished, as described above, the master put down his hammer. To me he then said: "Finish feeding and **(84)** clean the stables, then come and get your coffee." The ritual of drinking the coffee was always the same during those three and a half years. It was a coffee that I called "Apprenticeship Coffee." It was neither black and nor white. It was a dark undefinable brew and the same for its taste. The spread on the bread changed like a train's timetable: sausage lard, meat lard, bacon lard. The reason for that was: in the inn they used a lot of sausages because the entire traffic down from the mountains to Zwickau passed by our smithy. The majority of those people stopped by and got breakfast. For that reason, butchering took place every four weeks, and we were those who had to suffer from that, the maid and I.

Despite all our willingness, we were not able to cope with all that fatty food. At that time, I would have been happy if they had given me a little bit more of the jam that was served to us also according to a timetable. This monotony was interrupted only on Sundays. We did not get breakfast, but bread rolls with butter. Even the coffee was a bit clearer. The rest of the day was filled with work in the smithy, that means, to shoe the horses, or to repair the carts or plowing equipment. If there was not much work to do in the smithy, which occasionally happened, then I was busy chopping wood. Furthermore, there was always plenty of work to be done in the fields or in the garden.

During the summer, it was necessary to harvest clover in the early morning or in the evening. When the cesspool was full, I had to scoop the muck with a bucket out of the pool and carry it to the manure pile. Occasionally, this pile had to be leveled, too.

A unique chapter of my apprenticeship was the issue of sweeping the courtyard. It was situated in front of the smithy and the neighboring house, which also used to be an inn, as it was about 6 meters wide. This yard had to be swept every Sunday and before every holiday. As I have already mentioned, the entire transportation traffic made a stop at our place. At that time, the largest part of the vehicles was still drawn by horses. The coachmen took refreshments only so that the horses could get something to feed, or the other way around. At any rate, when a cart came by, the coachman placed the food in front of the horses or hung the holster around the horse's neck. Then, he went to the inn's restaurant. Once the horses had eaten the oats, they got hay and grass depending on the duration of the stop or on the coachman's personality or on the length of the entire trip.

(85) At that time, a picture hung in the general room of the inn. It showed an inn with a horse and a carriage in front of it. Below the inscription: "Here you stop and get a drink, to happily continue your journey over mountains and through valleys." This business traffic meant that at the end of the week the yard looked quite terrible. Often, I felt rather uncomfortable just thinking about sweeping the yard. Every time, I breathed a sigh of relief when I was done with it. Often the entire load of manure had the volume comparable to a whole horse cart. From one year to the next, I actually clocked 52 days of sweeping.

I had only a little bit of free time. On Saturdays, when the workers from the factories in Wilkau came by on their bikes or by the narrow-gauge railway train, it got really busy. On Sundays in the morning, I had to clean up the smithy. At noon, I fed the horses, then I got to eat. Often, I also had to polish all the shoes and fetch coal from the cellar for the kitchen. After lunch, I washed myself and got dressed. When I got my 50 *Pfennige* [70] salary from the master's wife, I ran on the double along the tracks of the narrow-gauge railway train to Wilkau, skipping from the railroad's tie to tie, got on a streetcar and went home. During my entire apprenticeship, it felt like a celebration to me getting a chance to visit home. My mother always had something special for me, either fresh-baked rolls or a big jug of milk. In the summer she gave me rolls and milk, cold, or a great bowl with rhubarb. I always had a great appetite.

Around 6 p.m., I had to leave again because I had to feed the animals in the evening. I was granted a vacation only once during the three and a half years, and this was only because I went with my father and mother to Roßlau [73] during Pentecost 1927. Although I had very little free time, there were also nice days. During hot summer evenings, I regularly went for a swim in the nearby Rödel-Bach [74] or in the streambed of the mill. The Haukenberg [75] was also a great opportunity to let off steam as typical for this age. It was wonderful to climb up the Haukenberg situated on the opposite side and from there to gaze over the entire landscape.

One could see deep below our smithy and the road, or watch the narrow-gauge train passing by. Everything was so small and cute. **(86)** It was also nice when I was asked to deliver the bills at the end of the month. I began in Niederhaßlau at the Kuntz mill. From there, I went over to Wilkau, Haara, all the way up to Wüsker Karl, my master's brother-in-law. That was already almost in Silberstraße. I walked back through the Lachsengrund, a romantic section of the forest. In the afternoon I walked the opposite direction: Cunersdorf, Niedercrinitz, Culitzsch.

These walks opened for me a better view of the forest and meadows. I was always delighted to see beautiful farms, animals, or well-plowed fields, as if they were my own. In my mind, I was thinking about the providence of farmers. As it is custom in the countryside, people are talking about one another. They talk about, for example, whether this man is a good farmer or a bad one, that man has debts or too many children. They talk, for instance, about someone who just married whom or they talk about pretty much everything. I can really say, I often was just by myself but I however never felt lonely. My thoughts always gave me inspiration and kept me occupied. The simplest things interested me or gave me enjoyment.

When I reflect back on the winter days, when it got dark early, it was so romantic in the smithy, with the flickering light of the fire in the forge in which the master toiled. There was also the shower of sparks of the iron heated up to whiteness; those were things that easily seduced me to delve into dreams.

Then came Christmas. In the afternoon on Christmas Eve, I began sweeping the yard and cleaned up the smithy. The master and the children were no longer to be seen. When I was done, I washed myself, and then it was time for dinner. The others already waited for me. Dinner began. Everyone sat around the big, round table in the kitchen. We always had roasted goose with dumplings and fruit as dessert. For this meal, I received, as an exception, half a liter of Bavarian beer and a piece of goose which was quite large. We enjoyed the meal with true devotion. The children did not sit still during the meal because they could not wait any longer for the gift giving ceremony. Once the dishes were done, we took the spiral stairs up to the living room. The candles on the Christmas tree were already lit.

We sang **(87)** the traditional Christmas song and then each of us was led to the place where his or her presents had been placed. My Christmas gift always consisted of primarily money, plus a few small things. On the first day of Christmas, I got twenty-five marks. This amount increased from year to year, each time by twenty-five marks. I did not stay for long on Christmas Eve. After I had thanked everyone, I grabbed my stuff, tucked it under my arm, and fast-walked home. I do not remember that I ever walked slowly.

(88) – Page 88 is blank.

(89) Sunday, June 16, 1946

One entire year in Metz I was just working. The time passed by both slowly and quickly. Where will I be within a year? Today it is a rainy day, just right to spend time in the room. The past week was actually filled with various events. I received two letters, both from Herbert. He writes rather understandably. He is active in the Free German Youth movement. I would not have expected anything else. In my estimation, this generation and our own face a gigantic political task. He describes for me, in a few words, the political and economic life at home. It does not look pretty, but it corresponds entirely with my own expectations. The party is lacking operatives with drive and purpose. This is quite understandable.

A great number of them were eliminated during the years since 1933. Many of the others were, despite their unreliability, drafted into the military and were placed in units that suffered great losses. Those who survived both are still imprisoned and only a few are at home. The majority of the German people, however, now expect from those in charge that they create ad-hoc blissful conditions, without making any effort to reflect upon the fact that one can't rely on just a handful of people to rebuild the country, as it is primarily the responsibility of the entire people that includes everyone. However, what is even more important, they do not even want to realize that we have lost the war and that all major German cities are in ruins. Many of them demonstrate a great naiveté in evaluating the conditions. Instead, they should demonstrate what they can do, or, when one observes that progress is being made, then one is willing to also participate.

There is an expression going around which one can hear a lot: "Once I am at home again, I will not care about anything anymore. What matters is having a job and living with and for my family." In addition, everyone expects that the enemy forces will make every effort to fix everything in the Reich. The level of damage to our education during the past years since the last World War is shocking. One rarely finds any high-level social and ethical thinking, not to mention actions. Egoism, materialism, and a childish need for public acknowledgement dominate. Everyone bargains over the simplest things. One must watch out not to be drawn into such social milieu more than would be good. And yet, I cannot avoid smiling **(90)** when I listen to these shallow conversations, or when I see how a person musters all of his intelligence in order to secure a piece of uniform or other types of clothing, or to just try hard to gain the possession of it.

If I did not believe that the good in people vastly supersedes the evil part, insofar as people are raised and directed responsibly, or, if necessary, are forced to it, it would be impossible for me to achieve anything of superior quality for the common good with this mush of folks. Seeing this with eyes that have been trained by the school of the party, one knows exactly the reasons for this contradictory behavior of the masses.

We do not say for nothing: "The lack of judgement of the masses will never break a sword's wit." Those are the classical examples that one witnesses during imprisonment on a daily basis and which one can also find everywhere outside of the camp's barbed wire fence. Therefore, we must not get tired. A solid legwork is needed, to shake up each person so he awakens, and one must over and over drill into their brains what is at stake. Everyone must understand that the criminal structure of the social order was responsible for the misery of the masses, a structure that is not willing to permit the working people to receive their rightful share for their work. For this social structure, the mass of people is only a product that is being used in this melting pot of industry and economy, just as lime and steel or machines are consumed.

A machine that is quite complicated and expensive is being taken care of and treated with greatest attention until it has amortized, according to the business calculation and the amount of the aimed-for profit, the costs for its purchase and maintenance. Then it will be replaced by a new and perhaps more modern machine and is then sold at a ridiculous low price. A person earns what he is supposed to get according to the tariff, as long as he has healthy bones to do the job. And not look at them as a matter of amortization and replacement. He is either healthy and hence capable of working, or he is sick and is therefore not needed. The difference however, is only that a healthy person needs food, drinking, and clothing, and a sick person needs the same if not more. But the latter does not receive any of it. From then on, he depends on the generosity of social institutions or other public mercy.

(91) The content of the second letter was even more important. Herbert turns to me with a request to give him my opinion regarding his choice of a job. Normally this would have been a matter that I would have liked to arrange myself right there and then. The condition is as follows: my wife is no longer able to sustain the costs for attending a higher level of school. The conditions have dramatically changed. As for money, they must be extremely parsimonious. The financial support which she receives does not seem to be huge. Even though I had not had any particular plans with the boy, I would have preferred if he had attended school until the final class. I am sure that there would have been an opportunity, if I had been at home.

Unfortunately, I also must attribute the outcome of this case to me being a prisoner of war. He writes to me that he is supposed to work at a mine, so that later he can become a foreman of miners. But he is probably pursuing this only for now to receive a ration card for workers. For me it is not easy, due to my present circumstances, to advise the boy and my wife. The possibilities to write are so limited that it is not possible to analyze this matter exhaustively, and then so many circumstances play a role that I possibly do not know. *not a miner*

As to one thing, I decided that he will not work as a miner, irrespective of the material reasons which speak in favor of it. He is not built for that. During one of my furloughs, I had already considered this question. Herbert had told us that a teacher had told him that he should become an actor. My wife laughed about it. I made her stop and afterwards seriously expressed my opinion. At that time, there still was war.

Today we have something like peace. Herbert is active in the newly founded youth movement. He is writing articles for the newspaper and the radio. Everything according to his own thinking. In addition, several people again confirmed his talent for theater.

He now wants to become a radio host. I gave him my approval for this. Whether this is right the future will tell. Maybe the imprisonment may not last much longer, and then I still can intervene with help. You just must be an optimist in every respect and hope that everything will turn out well. Of course, the selection of a job is not something casual. It is after all the foundation for the position which a person will later assume in his life.

As for the way this matter will financially turn out, I must entrust those at home.

(92) – Page 92 is blank.

(93) June 19, 1946

One can well say the times are improving. Today, I got a fourth letter. It was from Mrs. Müller and Marie. As I am delighted about any mail, but was especially happy about this one. Hardly anyone can comprehend how good it felt to receive news this way. But you will notice immediately who has preserved the clear understanding of a sharp mind over the last twelve years. Among other things, there was also unpleasant news contained in it, in the way that the landlord tried to secretly make my wife dislike the apartment. But I will give her a lesson. It is already unpleasant to sit here and to know that the family depends in every respect on the mercy of the government, and then this happens. On the other hand, it reveals the mindset of those former Nazis. Now I am only anxious to find out what my wife will write.

The children walk around barefoot because they do not have shoes. That is not as bad by itself. We also had to walk barefoot as children. In that regard we have never possessed too much in our lives. Yet, I could help in many respects if I would be home. But this cannot be the case currently. I have always thought how we as children were happy that we could wear wooden clogs in Winter. It was not ideal to walk in those. The snow stuck to them, and then it happened quite often that the upper part fell off. And then you stood on the street helplessly and you had to walk home in socks.

Our children will have to go through such hard times the same way we suffered when we were young. First, the war with its constraints, then the post-war period. We were also defeated. At that time, there were ten and eleven people sitting at a table. One herring had to suffice for everyone. Everyone got a small strip and on top of that two, three potatoes. The questions concerning food were always the center of the conversation. The main meal was cabbage. Many meals consisted often only of cabbage in various forms of preparation. On Sunday we had for instance cabbage potatoes, which were cabbage cut into squares, steamed with caraway seed and salt. Cabbage salad, cabbage shredded and steamed with vinegar. On top of it a few real potatoes and little meat broth. In the evening we had cabbage potato salad. This was cabbage cut in slices like potatoes and some potatoes mixed under.

Once at New Year's Eve our mother made the traditional **(94)** potato salad in the dishwashing bowl. It consisted of cabbage, beets, and potatoes. How we enjoyed it. Our life was just as in this war. We ate up huge portions and yet, after a short period we could eat again. An unpleasant side effect was the urination. The night chamber pot was never enough. Therefore, we had a bucket for this purpose in the room. How much did we desire at that time to get a real fill with bread! Sometimes when my mother was in the store, we quietly took the bread cutter out of the kitchen cupboard and adjusted it so that it cut very thin slices, so that no one would notice the change in the bread, and we cut very quickly. For this action, we counted very much on mother's diminished hearing.

Because there was so little bread, most of the families were fighting. Everyone claimed that the other one would eat more from the bread than was allowed. For this reason, everyone kept his bread under lock and key. This was the case for us at home as well. Otto and Kurt were apprentices at that time and were at the age when they always were hungry. But they also kept their bread for themselves. At that time there was enough because they rationed rigidly of course. On the contrary, they managed to save some bread.

The following I will not forget. Otto had an extra two-pound bread. With this bread under our arm, we walked one Sunday afternoon to one of Otto's work colleagues, who lived in the Planitzstrasse. This colleague also had several smaller siblings. Otto gave the bread as a gift to them. That means we all ate the bread together. That was really a feast.

Despite those years of hunger, I grew up big and strong. For that reason, I'm firmly convinced that my children will also survive this time without major lasting damage. I know what a human being can sustain. It is important that a person learns also in those early years to gain experience in order to recognize the absurdity of the social structure. When that is the case, then there will not be any hesitation to join the front at the decisive moment, which is willing and capable to bring an end to this absurdity by all available means.

(95) Now, let me tell you quickly something that happened about this time last year [45] which aggravated even the softest minds. That is the meal plan. The previous year when we were assigned to a work unit, we were so weak that it was possible for someone to 'blow the Lord's prayer through our cheeks' [76]. Every time when we left the camp and waited outside of the gate, the main theme was food, and hence, the meal plan. 'The soup was once again superb', or 'today I got a full bowl.' When food was handed out, everyone watched carefully at what soup-bucket they used the largest soup ladle. The difference was minimal. And yet everyone amassed around that bucket and no one at the other. They had to be forced to the other. We ate what was in our bowl and we licked it clean with a finger, and the next thing was that one said, "Now I would like to eat another bowl." No one can believe what a famished person can devour. How often has it happened that someone had gotten some extra food and devoured it up until he had to vomit. In this regard, the human being does not differ in any way from the animal.

The normal meal plan was: in the morning, ten to fifteen biscuits or a quarter white bread and coffee. At noon, a liter of vegetable soup and red beets or vegetable salad. In the evening, a liter of corn milk soup, ten to fifteen biscuits or bread and coffee. At times, we got an extra portion. That means you got double the portion. Of course, this happened at noon or in the evening. These quantities we devoured without difficulties, with coffee and all the rest. When there was a second portion, you also finished that. On the contrary, we would have even eaten more.

I once managed to eat four portions of bean soup and twenty-five biscuits with coffee. The circumstances required that I had to eat whatever I could force into myself. I was not allowed to keep anything, and I also could not give a share to another fellow prisoner because I ate all this in the kitchen of another company, in which I had done some odd job. When I then left the kitchen, I was afraid. With every step I feared that I might vomit again. I immediately went to our accommodations and lay down on the bed and then I wheezed like a dying person. I pledged to myself: never again!

(96) This was a comment just on the side. At any rate, not long after dinner a pilgrimage began to the bulletin board at which was attached the meal plan. First, we studied the one for our own company, then those of the other four companies. The results were compared and discussed. The kitchen staff was more or less ridiculed and criticized. Often during the dinner someone entered and called "man, tomorrow we will have a fantastic menu." He told us the content of the menu. Nevertheless, everyone went outside to check it himself and thus to be able to look forward to the next day twice as much.

To mention the various stages of action that took place around the food menu would probably be worthy to describe, but it would fill several pages, and I do not want to do this today. Anyway, this condition lasted until Christmas. Then it petered out. Today the thing is, if one asks what we will have to eat tomorrow, then certainly no one would know.

For memory's sake I want to record the menu of one week:

Monday, June 17, 1946

Breakfast: one quarter bread, jam, coffee

Lunch: bean stew with sausages

Dinner: vegetable stew, scrambled eggs, one quarter bread, coffee

Tuesday, June 18, 1946

Breakfast: one quarter bread, cheese, coffee

Lunch: three dumplings, goulash, carrots, corn compote

Dinner: three quarter liter milk soup, fishcake, one quarter bread, coffee

Wednesday, April [June] 19, 1946

Breakfast: one quarter bread, jam, coffee

Lunch: boiled potatoes, goulash, cabbage

Dinner: fried potatoes, scrambled eggs, one quarter bread, coffee

Thursday, April [June] 20, 1946

Breakfast: one quarter bread, jam, coffee

Lunch: bean stew, a slice of bread

Dinner: milk soup, quiche, one quarter bread, coffee

Friday, April [June] 21, 1946

Breakfast:

(97) Elsterhorst [77], July 25, 1946

The imprisonment comes to an end. How often have we discussed the question of our release, and examined the When, How, and Where. Now we have the answer. I will try to describe the individual steps. During the last days of the month of June, more and more rumors emerged concerning releases. Considering the end stage of our work project, this was very possible.

Very suddenly, they created a list of those who were to be released. For the most part, those who were married and those who were older ones amongst the singles were on the list. Nevertheless, there was strong disbelief and pessimism. From then on, all kinds of specific dates were mentioned when it was supposed to happen. None applied.

Finally, on Saturday, June 29, the leader of the company announced the names and the date. This news immediately triggered a change in the mood of the PWs [43]. This evening, people sang songs and played music endlessly. The following

Sunday people everywhere were busily packing up and made all necessary preparations.

One Monday July 1st, it finally started. At seven o'clock everyone stood in the yard with his gear. There were about four hundred people from our camp. We had to stand at attention, count, names were read out loud, several times, and had to wait a long time. At 9 a.m. we marched out of the gate and got onto the trucks. As far as we were concerned, it could start immediately. But everything requires time. After we had waited for a whole hour, we finally started. We drove through the city of Metz. Trucks from two other camps joined us.

At the end we were a convoy of about forty trucks. And now we left the city. The route took us via Etain, Reims – Soissons – Attichy [78]. The weather was great, almost too good. The sun was very hot. At the beginning of the ride, everyone was excited and full of expectations. Eventually one after the other began to fall asleep. We were soaked with sweat and dirty when we arrived. At the arrival many felt awkward. The camp reminded us too much of Ludwigshafen and Stenay. Now it was Atychie (or Atichy?) [78].

We were tired like dogs and thirsty. If we believed that we could immediately go to our accommodations, we felt cheated. Immediately the marching began from one camp to another. "Pick up your gear, put down your gear." Following the rhythm of these commands, we moved forward in snatches. After all, we were 1,500 men, and it did not go so quickly to bring those who were properly counted to their right places during a gloomy night.

(98) The worst of it all was the back and forth transporting the gear. Although we had already taken out everything that was superfluous while we were still in the camp, it got heavier and heavier.

The first night we rested in the release camp. We slept in tents. One tent for fifteen men and we had nice cots. We slept like the gods. In the morning we had our first meal. One third bread and soup. At noon we got vegetable soup. In comparison to the prisoner camp, it was less food but we got enough. During the day, we had the usual daily routine in a prisoner camp: count, establishment of work units, and similar things.

In the afternoon we had already left this camp and gone to the camp's checkpoint [79]. Everyone had to fill out a questionnaire and was questioned regarding his membership in the ⚡⚡ [4]. The next step was that they examined our bags and suitcases. In the evening, we ended up in a new camp. In this camp, different categories of people were selected. First, volunteers for the police. Then people for the core [80] and at last those who were politically suspicious. We felt as if we were on a sifter.

Everyone breathed a sigh of relief when we left this camp. Now we moved into the zoning cage [81], now we are through. The danger that someone still might be taken out no longer existed. But it could happen that someone was removed from the various transports because he had been guilty of breaking the sacred camp order. Nevertheless, everyone was nervous because no one could wait for the transport. At first, we had to fill out some forms, such as release from the *Wehrmacht* [82] and the handing out of money.

Finally, a transport of 1,200 men was assembled. Everyone asked everyone else whether he knew when it was to start. Very suddenly there was the order that the transport A27 will be ready tomorrow morning Friday on July 12, with gear, exactly at 9 a.m. ready for the departure. Everyone was feverish, everywhere there was joyous excitement. Again, we faced a new stage. Friday began. Exactly at 9 a.m. the group was ready. It began with counting and ended with counting. At first again we had to go to the camp's checkpoint [79]. We had to line up alphabetically. All the stuff was examined, the certificate for the money we had earned was handed over. The action was done. Now we were waiting until 7:30 p.m. Altogether the entire action lasted from 10 a.m. until the evening. Just a little bit had been needed for us to fall back into pessimism if the order to depart had not been issued. Despite the heavy gear we raced out of the gate.

(99) Consequently, our way went into the mountains. After an hour's march, we reached the train station of Atichy [78]. We arrived soaked with sweat. The train was already there. In the order we arrived, we got into the cars. Always 42 men together. It did not take long until the engine was attached and off, we went. Now it was clear that we were going home.

The ride took us once again across France. Direction west to east. Friday evening, we had been loaded onto the train cars and, on Sunday afternoon, we arrived in Bebra. The major towns where we stopped were: Soissons, Montmédy, Diedenhofen, Metz, Straßburg, Kehl, Karlsruhe, Mannheim, Frankfurt, Hanau, Fulda.

In Bebra everyone got off. The train then returned to Atichy [78]. Technically we were already free. The first thing that we did was to purchase a beer. The continuing transport to the Russian sector depended on diverse formalities. Consequently, we were placed into train cars until Monday located on a holding rail track. On Monday afternoon the transport to Eisenach began. At a small train station between Bebra and Eisenach we were handed over to the Russians. *handed over to Russian*

In Eisenach we were briefly welcomed, then we marched to the first quarantine camp. We were examined, registered, and released. This was a matter that lasted till the night. The following day we were resting everywhere in the camp and waited for the further transport to Erfurt. In the evening it started. We arrived in Erfurt at night. At night we were registered, examined, and deloused. Then we were led into a camp outside of the city. They told us that we would get away from here within 24, at latest, 48 hours. After 3 ½ days, on a Saturday afternoon, we continued with our ride. In the evening the train left that was going to take us now to the 3rd and last camp in Hoyerswerda. During the ride we took a detour via Torgau, Pretzsch.

On Sunday evening we arrived in Hoyerswerda. Here again, the registration, the release, and examination lasted until midnight. Here they also announced that the quarantine would last 16 days, together with the arrival and departure days.

Today I am waiting for my transport. Due to special circumstances, this one is also delayed, so I will probably be able to finally leave tomorrow on August 6 and will thus complete the chapter of the imprisonment.

(100) – Page 100 is blank.

EPILOGUE

ON JANUARY 3, 1933 – JUST A FEW WEEKS BEFORE THE THEN German President Paul von Hindenburg names Adolf Hitler as chancellor of Germany, my great-grandmother Meta Häber (mother of Fritz) writes in her diary: "Today is demonstration by communists. All are there, except Hanne and Anna. Hulda writes that they also voted for the communists. *Therefore, they cannot blame one another.*"

Her conclusion confirmed for me – as it did for generations of my family throughout history – that there is always a choice to do something or to – at least – acknowledge or to do nothing and look the other way when evil occurs.

My grandfather, Fritz Häber, begins his diary with a dedication to his family: "I dedicate these pages to my wife and my children of whom I hope are still alive and whom to find well when I return from captivity." His unbowed, strong belief in his survival gave him faith to see his family again one day. Having endured physical and emotional challenges, my grandfather's story will inspire future generations, as it does for me today, almost 80 years later. I felt that, through his diary, he was able to spin an invisible thread of hope despite his struggling circumstances, no matter how hopeless they seemed.

I admire my grandfather for his resilience throughout his entire life. By working on this publication, I have gained so much more insight into his life and my family's history. It has revealed many —some surprising— parallels to my life living in the United States during the first quarter of the 21st century. For example, during the 45th presidency, we combatted a rising populism that, over the course of those four years, had the potential of leading to an authoritative dictatorship like in Germany in the 1930s.

My grandfather's cursive handwriting in the original diary is remarkably immaculate. His way of storytelling is easy to follow, and his descriptions take the reader's imagination directly to the location of the action. For me, the narrative reads like a novel and turns this book into a thrilling page-turner.

humor

I also appreciate his deadpan humor that he flashed out of the blue. During my recorded interview, speaking in his strong Saxonian accent, he made fun of the regional Nazi government. In the 1930s, a county in Germany was called *Gau* led by a *Gauleiter* (county leader). As an admirer of wordplay, Fritz considered himself a *Gaul-Leiter* (*Gaul* = German for horse) in his own right as he, working for a local farmer, led a cart pulled by a horse to transport products to various places in town.

This diary of my grandfather, the diaries of my great-grandmother, as well as the tape-recorded interviews with both my grandfather and my father allow me to draw from a well of stories and to assemble the pieces of my family history. Compared to many historical accounts about life during wartime, my ancestors were not afraid to share sincere accounts of how their lives were back then, excluding literary frills and unnecessary decoration.

Lastly, I am very thankful for my grandfather's exhaustive research of our family history. Tracing records back to the 17th century, he found an entry in the archives of a church near Zwickau in Saxony, stating that someone had changed our last name from Häberer to Häber at one point. Because of that, I know that any person carrying Häber as a last name is likely related to me and my family.

I would like to leave readers with a note from Herbert Häber, my father and eldest son of Fritz, who, after I decided to publish his father's diary, shared a sentiment with me. Just a few weeks before he passed away in April 2020, he remembered having sent letters as a 15-year-old to his father in the POW camp in France but did not remember what he had written. He stated: "Having now had a chance to read my father's references to these letters in his diary reminded me of how my occupational history came about. Thankfully, he had decided for me to neither become a coal miner nor an actor, but eventually, a journalist as he recognized my sophisticated use of the German language in my writing. And for that, I will eternally be thankful to him."

In loving memory!
Bernd Häber, January 2024, Phoenix, Arizona/USA

Appendices

MAPS

MAP 1: Zwickau in Saxony/Germany and surrounding
locations which Fritz mentioned in the diary.

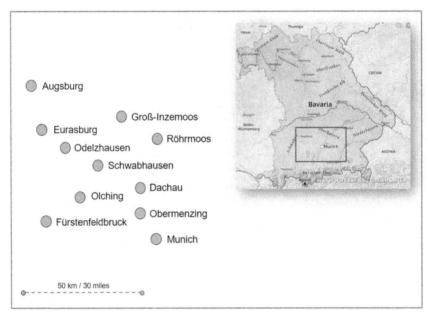

MAP 2: Munich in Bavaria/Germany and surrounding locations mentioned in the diary.

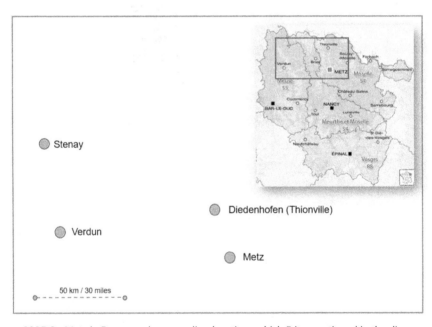

MAP 3: Metz in France and surrounding locations which Fritz mentioned in the diary.

LETTER FROM UWE HÄBER

My Second Chance

GRANDPARENTS. THEY GREW UP TOGETHER WITH US, SHARED in many moments of our lives. Memories still present, and yet, already faded. As we have grown up, the questions that we want to ask them today are different. However, they are not with us anymore. All stories of their childhood and adolescence, adventures of their time, irretrievably gone!

I did not dare ask them.

Not because I did not feel like asking them, but because I was just too young and too busy with my life. Memories of war were, as for many other families, not a subject. The today and the now were as predominant as was forgetting and suppressing the other things. Perhaps, we did not ask because we thought that there were no big stories from our ordinary grandparents. They were just Grandma and Grandpa to us – what's there to document anyway?

The generation of my – our – grandparents, however, has stories to offer, rather than getting them from history books. Born during the German Empire, World War I, Weimar Republic, Great Depression, National Socialism and Fascism, World War II, captivity as prisoner of war, death, destruction – it all influenced their childhood and adolescence and shaped their personality. This was then followed by a new Germany after 1945, occupation by the Allied Forces, the founding of the German Democratic Republic (GDR) in the zone occupied by the Soviets, socialism per the Stalinist dictate, a centrally planned economy, one-party ruling, glasnost and perestroika, the fall of the Berlin Wall in 1989, and the German reunification.

What a century!

And all of this in a single lifetime; this was the life of our grandparents – and yet, I did not bother asking.

103

Nonetheless, there are these diary notes – a personal documentation, a recorded life – the life of my grandfather, Fritz Häber. Excerpts and insight into both contemporary and family history. Memories by my grandfather of times that we only can begin to fathom what it had meant to experience, to live through, and to survive times of war with all its abysmal ugliness. What anguish, what courage, what strength was needed, I cannot say – because I did not dare asking.

And yet today, 75 years later, we hold his diary in our hands. Why did he write it? Did he do it for himself or did he want to say, "This is how it was then; this is what I had to go through – do not forget about these times, never!"

At this point, I would like to quote Elie Wiesel, who survived the Holocaust and had received the Nobel Peace Prize in 1986: "Without memory, there is no culture. Without memory, there would be no civilization, no society, no future."

In memory of my grandfather, this book is, therefore, my second chance to connect with him once more.

Uwe Häber (grandson of Fritz) – written in 2021

LETTER FROM HANS HÄBER

WHO WAS FRITZ HÄBER? HE WAS MY BIOLOGICAL FATHER. I was the sixth of seven children in our family – six boys and one girl. Being at an old age now and having been a miner, a farmer, and a journalist throughout my long, professional life, I realized early on that my father was, first and foremost, a German Communist. Not like the official "textbook version" as often portrayed in history books, but one who genuinely wanted - again and again, no matter life's circumstance – to demonstrate his conviction in word and deed, free from "hollow phrases" that were quite common in the GDR.

Essentially, Fritz Häber was a Communist since 1954 without flaunting the party membership book. Rather, he was one with a good heart and a clear mind as he genuinely believed in Marx and Lenin - the godfathers of the Communist movement. During 1954, his fellow party comrades labeled him, in a blunt Stalinist manner, a "traitor of the cause" for having taken part in a shooting squad, acting under order, during his time as a soldier in the *Wehrmacht*. They conveniently overlooked the fact that – at that time during the war – he was suspected of spreading Communist propaganda, which was punishable under martial law. Serendipitously, it never came to a trial because the Third Reich collapsed shortly thereafter, due to the advancement of the American and Russian armies on German soil.

After he got expelled from the party in 1954, he proved himself through work as he, in his earlier days, had learned smithery when he worked twelve-hour days. Following the expulsion, Fritz, as the "disgraced one", demonstrated that he could work hard in a fettling shop in Zwickau, a back-breaking job. He had no other choice; he had seven hungry children at home. A few years later, he found work as a miner in a black coal mine. Every day, he went underground, more than 1,000 meters deep, and worked as a coal hewer to earn a decent wage.

As a person, he did not cave in at all. Quite the contrary; he soon became one of the most productive workers and was given the "activist of socialist labor" award. Repeatedly, he voiced concerns about drawbacks and sloppiness in the underground workplace. He wrote articles in the house journal *Grubenlampe* (a miner's headlamp). As a result, the foreman of miners, his boss, held Fritz in high regard.

The company's leaders and senior party officials responded quite differently. Just to show who was in charge, they shot down his application for re-entry into the Communist movement and party, the East-German Socialist Unity Party of Germany (SED), using tacky arguments. He, as the rejected one, continued to be the expelled one. It did not deter Fritz from continuing to stay strong and to hold up his ideals.

Good work does ennoble one – this was his firm conviction of dignity and being human. Thus, his sons had to enter the working world as he once did. Higher education was not affordable but rather something left to their own initiative. Working during the day and studying in the evening, the oldest son became a journalist, one became a lathe operator, and his other three sons became miners like him with me one of the latter. The youngest became a machinist and later a train engine-driver.

One episode, when he was in his early 60s after he had retired as a miner, shows how strong my father's work ethics were. He worked a part-time job at a beer brewery in Zwickau and was in charge of the boiler house. During one nightshift, the boiler house started to "shake" - but also his heart. Instead of calling for a doctor, he continued working. In order to lessen the pain in his heart, he laid down on top of the boiler, to "warm his heart and soul", and stayed there until the end of his shift in the early morning. Then, he took his bicycle and cycled home. From there, he rode to the closest hospital, which was 10 kilometers away, and checked in. Diagnosis:

Reasonable suspicion of an infarction! There, they decommissioned him immediately.

Books and reading were a major part of his life. One of his friends in elementary school was 'Moppel' – a tiny pencil that helped him master the basic math arithmetic and reading skills. Books were his universities and therefore, always companions, no matter where he was: bathtub, vacation trip, tramway, train, bus, airplane or hospital. He was hungry for literature and eager to read everything published. Most importantly, he consumed literature of the GDR, from writers like Bertolt Brecht, Willi Bredel, Thomas and Heinrich Mann, Bruno Apitz, Arnold Zweig, Erich Weinert, Ludwig Renn, and Alfred Kurella, as they were heroes of antifascism. Also, he read classic GDR-authors, such as Erwin and Eva Strittmatter, Christa Wolf, Erik Neutsch, and Hermann Kant. He did not shy away from the old and new Russian texts: Tolstoi, Dostojewski, Turgeniew, Gorki, Scholochow, Ostrowski, Aitmatow, Fadejew, Ehrenburg, and many more. Last but not least, he also read books from American authors when released in the GDR, such as Mark Twain, Jack London, William Faulkner, and Ernest Hemingway.

He kept reading until the very end of his life, which was accompanied by the demise of the Soviet Union, the fatherland of communism and its adopted child the GDR - a country that Fritz helped launch knowing what capitalism really was. A country that, after 40 years of state-directed economy, was dismissed by its citizens overnight, with the hope for more freedom, democracy, and a free market economy. For Fritz Häber, the antifascist and Communist, now being a citizen of West-Germany, this "lost country" was very difficult to accept. As for some of the East-German political leaders who repudiated clemency issued by the new and old historic victors, who tried to run away and ended up in prison, and who died in emigration, there was no escape from responsibility. As for Fritz Häber, it was one more final run of repeated history until he passed away in 1998.

Hans Häber (son of Fritz) – written in 2021

PHOTOS

Fritz as a Wehrmacht soldier (year unknown - likely taken between 1941 and 1945).

Die Eltern, ich und der Hund Mucki.
1920

Fritz with his mother Meta and his father Emil and his dog Mucki in 1920.

Fritz (as toddler in front) with his mother Meta and his father Emil, his
brothers Kurt and Otto (twin brothers to the left and right), a cousin Marie,
his sister Anna (with glasses) and his sister Lene (next to him) in 1912.

Fritz's family in likely 1941 (6 of 7 children); Left to right: Karl, Kurt, Herbert (oldest son), Lore, Linda (wife), Hans and Peter; Fritz jr. was born in 1944.

Left to right: Fritz as wrestler (likely early 1930s). Fritz was a hard-working man in every profession he held.

Fritz as POW working as a welder in an American car repair shop in June of 1945.

Fritz (in the back with cap) at farmer Arno Schmidt's
farm after his release from prison in 1934.

Fritz (right) as a mechanic (Montagehelfer) at Thyssen-Dresden
constructing a factory building for the Auto Union in 1935.

Fritz loved smoking cigars (picture taken likely in the 1950s).

Fritz with farmer Schmidt's horse - related to the Gaul-Leiter story.

Fritz as senior citizen (at the time of the tape-recorded interview in 1990).

Fritz among his extended family in East-Germany (likely in the 1950s) with his sister Anna (center with glasses).

Left to right: Emil – father of Fritz – in his younger years, and Meta – mother of Fritz – in her younger years.

DOCUMENTS

Certificate of Journeyman's Examination for Fritz as Blacksmith (issued in October 1927).

Certificate of Church Confirmation for Fritz (issued in April 1924
by the Evangelic-Lutheran Church in Zwickau/Saxony).

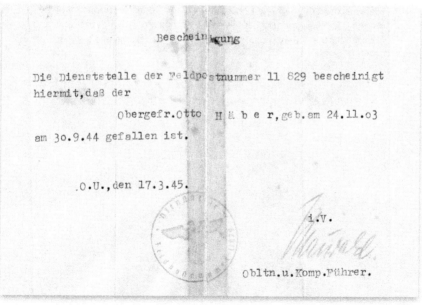

Original attestation of death for Otto Häber (brother of Fritz) who was killed
in battle in September 1944 (issued by the Wehrmacht in March 1945).

117

Meta Häber – Entry (lines underscored by her) in her diary on January 3, 1933: On January 3, 1933 – just a few weeks before the then German President Paul von Hindenburg names Adolf Hitler as chancellor of Germany, my great-grandmother Meta Häber (mother of Fritz) writes in her diary: "Today is demonstration by communists. All are there, except Hanne and Anna. Hulda writes that they also voted for the communists. Therefore, they cannot blame one another."

WARNING
Warnung

— Anyone who supplies, or puts his signature to, false particulars, or who falsifies entries or signatures will be subject to

THE MOST SEVERE PENALTIES

Wer falsche angaben macht, diese unterzeichnet oder Eintragungen oder Unterschriften fälscht oder verfälscht

WIRD SCHWER BESTRAFT

To be completed by the person to whom this form relates.

CERTIFICATION
Erklärung

Auszufüllen durch die Person, auf die diese Karte sich bezieht.

I, (NAME OF UNDERSIGNED)
Ich, (Name des Unterzeichneten)

HAEBER   FRITZ

hereby certify that, to the best of my knowledge and belief, the particulars given on the front of this form are true.

erkläre hiermit, nach bestem Wissen und Gewissen, dass die umseitigen Angaben wahr sind.

SIGNATURE,

Fritz Haber

Unterschrift,

To be completed by the commander of the unit or formation rendering this form.

AUTHENTICATION
Beglaubung

Auszufertigen durch den Offizier der den Truppenteil befehligt.

I certify that the particulars on the front of this form have been checked against all documents available to me. I further certify that, to the best of my knowledge and belief they are correct and that the above signature is that of the individual concerned.

Ich bestätige hiermit dass ich alle umseitigen Angaben mit den mir zur Verfügung stehenden Papieren verglichen habe. Ich bestätige ausserdem, dass diese Angaben richtig sind und die obergenannten Person die vorstehende Erklärung eigenhändig unterzeichnet hat.

FRANK A. EVERITT
1st Lt. Inf.

SIGNATURE,

Unterschrift,

DATE   *OCTOBER 27 1945*   JUL 10 1946
Datum

LEF. - 1289-5-45/6.000.000/78034

Affidavit of Fritz certifying that he told nothing but the truth about his military services authorized by the Americans.

Concentration camp release paper (official certificate) from May 4, 1933.

Ausfertigung.   2

Polizeidirektion Zwickau   Zwickau, den 15. Juni 1933.

Konten:
Sächsische Staatsbank Zwickau
Konto Nr. 115186 der Sächs. Staatsbank Zwickau   Herrn
bei dem Postscheckamt Leipzig
Zwickauer Stadtbank Nr. 1666   Fritz   H ä b e r ,
Postschließfach 179
Fernruf: Sammelnummer 5141   . Schmied, ...

Geschäftszeichen:
5200/2.   ~~Bzw. im Konzentrationslager Sclob Osterstein~~
                           z.Zt. im Polizeigefängnis

                                          in   Z w i c k a u .
                                          - - - - - - - - -

            Sie $\frac{sind}{haben}$ am 26. Mai 1933 unter dem Verdacht
in Schutzhaft genommen worden, Ihrem in Dresden wohnenden
Bruder Kurt in der Verbindung mit der hiesigen U.B.-Leitung
der K.P.D. Hilfsdienste geleistet und damit die nationalen
Interessen auf das Schwerste gefährdet zu haben. Die Ver-
hängung der Schutzhaft gründet sich auf § 1 der Verordnung
des Reichspräsidenten zum Schutz von Volk und Staat vom
28. Februar 1933.

    . .   . .

            ~~Ihre Betätigung im bisherigen Sinne bildet also~~
~~eine Gefährdung der nationalen Interessen, demnach § 1~~
~~der Verordnung des Reichspräsidenten zum Schutz von~~
~~Volk und Staat vom 28. Februar 1933 ist daher die Schutz-~~
~~haft über Sie verhängt worden.~~ Sie erhalten Nachricht,
sobald diese Maßnahme wieder aufgehoben wird.

                    D i e   P o l i z e i d i r e k t i o n .

                    (gez.)   D ü n n e b i e r .

                         Polizeidirektor.

                    Ausgefertigt:
            Zwickau, am 16. Juni 1933.

            Oberreg.-Inr.

126.5.33.200.

Written confirmation that he was taken in to protective custody on May 26, 1933 charging
him with 'endangering the social order due to his support of the communist movement'.

S.Reg.1609/33
O.St.A.III 308/33

Abschrift !

H a f t b e f e h l.

1.) Der am 13.Juni 1894 in Halle geborene

Elektromonteur Willy Karl Robert S c h m i d t ,

2.) der am 2.August 1906 in Zwickau/Sa geborene

Othopädie-Mechaniker Hermann K e l l e r ,

3.) der am 2.Februar 1870 in Neustädtel b./Schneeberg gebore-

ne Berginvalid Franz Bernhard Z i m m e r m a n n

und

4.) der am 22.Januar 1910 in Leipzig geborene

Schmied Fritz Ehrenfried H ä b e r

sind zur Untersuchungshaft zu bringen.

Sie sind verdächtigt,

das Unternehmen,die Verfassung des Deutschen Reiches gewalt-

sam zu ändern,dadurch vorbereitet zu haben,daß sie in der

Zeit von März bis Ende Mai 1933 u.a.in Dresden und Zwickau

die Organisation der KPD teils durch brieflichen Verkehr

teils durch persönliche Verbindung aufrecht erhielten und

dadurch bewußt den gewaltsamen Sturz der Verfassung anstreb-

ten.

- Verbrechen nach §§ 86,81 Ziffer 2 St.G.B. -

Die Untersuchungshaft wird verhängt,

weil ein Verbrechen den Gegenstand der Untersuchung bildet,

somit Fluchtverdacht besteht.Überdies besteht Verdunkelungs-

Indictment (page 1) from August 18, 1933 charging him with
'overturning the constitutional order by violence'.

gefahr,da außer den in Haft befindlichen Beschuldigten noch andere Teilnehmer vorhanden sind,deren Aufenthalt noch nicht ermittelt ist.

Gegen diesem Haftbefehl ist das Rechtsmittel der Be schwerde zulässig.

Statt der Beschwerde kann mündliche Verhandlung übe den Haftbefehl beantragt werden.

Zwickau,den 18. August 1933.

Das Amtsgericht.

Dr.v.Großmann

Der Urkundsbeamte
der Geschäftsstelle bei dem Amtsgericht Zwickau.

Indictment (page 2) from August 18, 1933 charging him with
'overturning the constitutional order by violence'.

Writ of summons for Fritz to appear in front of a judge
on May 24, 1934 charging him with treason.

Aus meinem Leben!

1. Willi Mittenzwey, Schmiedelehrling von April 1924 bis
   Culitzsch b. Wilkau   September 1927
   bei Kost m. Logis Lohn: 1. Jahr 0,50 M pro Woche
                            2. "   1.00 " "   "
                            3. "   1,50 " "   "
                   letztes Halbjahr 3,00 " "   "

2. Schmiedemeister   Schmiedegeselle   Oktober 1927
   in Niederalbersdorf
   bei Kost und Logis 7,50 M pro Woche, mit dem Sohn in einem
   Bett geschlafen.

3. Schmiedemeister, Otto Richter. Ohne Kost und Logis 28,00 M
   Eckersbach   pro Woche.
   Ein Fahrrad für 170,00 M auf Abzahlung gekauft. Wochenrate 5,-M.
   Von Nov. 1927 bis Sept. 1928.

4. Schmiedemeister Kändler,   14 Tage   7,- M die Woche
   Langenhessen b. Werdau.   Kost u. Logis

5. Schmidemeister Johannes König. Oktober 1928 - Januar 1929
   Zwickau   Wochenlohn 30,- M

6.   Stahlwerksarbeiter
   Zwickau-Lichtentanne.   Nach 14 Tagen wurde die Belegschaft
                               gewissermaßen beurlaubt, da die
                               Belegschaft in Unterwellenborn streikte
                               keine Zuschlagstoffe von dort kamen.

Compilation of Jobs for Fritz (documented by Fritz) including
references to salary (listed as board & lodging).

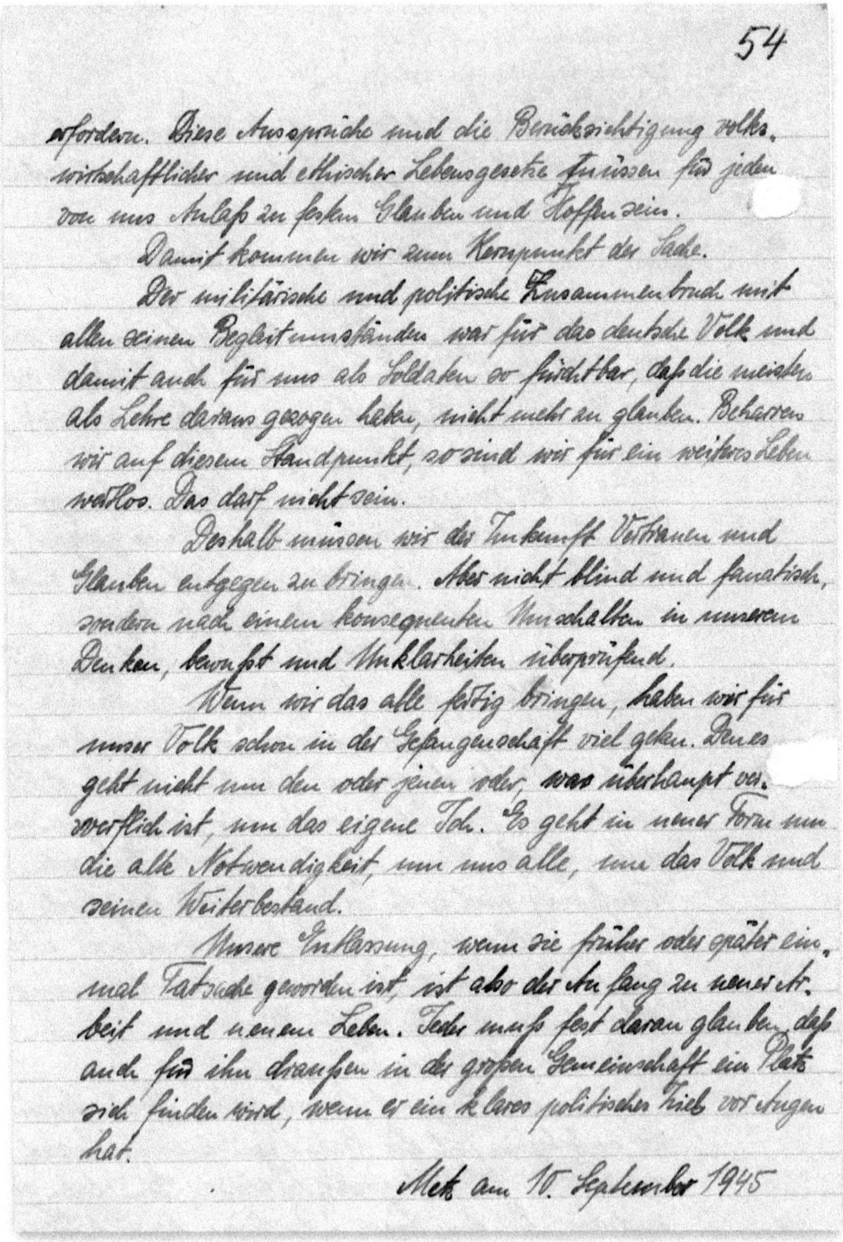
54

erfordern. Diese Aussprüche und die Berücksichtigung volks-
wirtschaftlicher und ethischer Lebensgesetze müssen für jeden
von uns Anlaß zu festem Glauben und Hoffen sein.

Damit kommen wir zum Kernpunkt der Sache.

Der militärische und politische Zusammenbruch mit
allen seinen Begleitumständen war für das deutsche Volk und
damit auch für uns als Soldaten so furchtbar, daß die meisten
als Lehre daraus gezogen haben, nicht mehr zu glauben. Beharren
wir auf diesem Standpunkt, so sind wir für ein weiteres Leben
wertlos. Das darf nicht sein.

Deshalb müssen wir der Zukunft Vertrauen und
Glauben entgegen zu bringen. Aber nicht blind und fanatisch,
sondern nach einem konsequenten Umschalten in unserem
Denken, bewußt und Unklarheiten überprüfend.

Wenn wir das alle fertig bringen, haben wir für
unser Volk schon in der Gefangenschaft viel getan. Denn es
geht nicht um den oder jenen oder, was überhaupt ver-
werflich ist, um das eigene Ich. Es geht in neuer Form um
die alte Notwendigkeit, um uns alle, um das Volk und
seinen Weiterbestand.

Unsere Entlassung, wenn sie früher oder später ein-
mal Tatsache geworden ist, ist also der Anfang zu neuer Ar-
beit und neuem Leben. Jeder muß fest daran glauben, daß
auch für ihn draußen in der großen Gemeinschaft ein Platz
sich finden wird, wenn er ein klares politisches Ziel vor Augen
hat.

Metz am 10. September 1945

Page 54 of the original diary ("Let us get to the essence of it. The military and political collapse with all its accompanying circumstances was so horrible for both the German people and us as soldiers that the majority of people stopped believing in anything. If we are to continue with such an attitude, life would not be worth living. This cannot be.").

ENDNOTES

[1] Stenay - town northeast of Reims

[2] Dachau - town in 'Upper Bavaria district of Bavaria, a state in the southern part of Germany. It is a major district town of the administrative region of Upper Bavaria, about 12 miles north-west of Munich.' Dachau was also the location of 'a Nazi concentration camp opened on 22 March 1933, which was initially intended to hold political prisoners. ... Its purpose was enlarged to include forced labor, and, eventually, the imprisonment of Jews, German and Austrian criminals, and finally foreign nationals from countries that Germany occupied or invaded. ... The main camp was liberated by U.S. forces on 29 April 1945.' https://en.wikipedia.org/wiki/Dachau,_Bavaria & https://en.wikipedia.org/wiki/Dachau_concentration_camp

[3] Röhrmoos and Groß-Inzemoos – two towns north of Dachau

[4] The Schutzstaffel (SS; also stylized as ᚻᚻ with Armanen runes; literally 'Protection Squadron') was a major paramilitary organization under Adolf Hitler and the Nazi Party (NSDAP) in Nazi Germany, and later throughout German-occupied Europe during World War II. It began with a small guard unit known as the Saal-Schutz ("Hall Security") made up of NSDAP volunteers to provide security for party meetings in Munich. In 1925, Heinrich Himmler joined the unit, which had by then been reformed and given its final name. Under his direction (1929–1945) it grew from a small paramilitary formation during the Weimar Republic to one of the most powerful organizations in Nazi Germany. From 1929 until the regime's collapse in 1945, the SS was the foremost agency of security, surveillance, and terror within Germany and German-occupied Europe. https://en.wikipedia.org/wiki/Schutzstaffel

[5] Likely meant to say "Krönung" as reference to be awarded.

[6] Kirchweihfest – Annual religious festivity celebrated in the Fall, similar to Octoberfest and Thanksgiving

[7] Free use of a German proverb indicating that 'even if a coachman seems to be in charge steering the coach wagon there is somehow a more supreme power that does the actual thinking' – he likely meant quote the German proverb "Men do the thinking but God does the steering"

[8] Kommissbrot, also Kommißbrot, is a dark type of German bread, baked from rye and other flours, historically used for military provisions. https://en.wikipedia.org/wiki/Kommissbrot

[9] Friedrichshafen - town at the north shore of Lake Constance

[10] RAD - The Reich Labor Service (Reichsarbeitsdienst; RAD) was a major organization established in Nazi Germany as an agency to help mitigate the effects of unemployment on the German economy, militarize the workforce and indoctrinate it with Nazi ideology. It was the official state labor service, divided into separate sections for men and women. https://en.wikipedia.org/wiki/Reich_Labour_Service

[11] Reference to a very detailed and bureaucratic system of technical rules

[12] Reference to an arrogant braggart, comparing such a person with a young deer pretending to having a mighty antler

[13] Refers to Fritz's employment at farmer Arno Schmidt's farm after his release from prison in 1934 when he was in charge of the horse and was distributing goods from the farm to people in the city and region.

[14] Fritz is mixing two ballads of Friedrich Schiller "Der Taucher" and "Das Lied von der Glocke".

[15] Pößneck - town south of Gera

[16] Friedberg - town east of Augsburg

[17] Use of the German proverb 'Farbe bekennen' as telling the truth, producing evidence or admitting to be wrong

[18] Odelzhausen - town north of Fürstenfeldbruck & northwest of Dachau

[19] Fritz refers to the year 1945

[20] Fritz was born on January 10, 1910

[21] Reference to the NSDAP (National Socialist German Workers' Party); The National Socialist German Workers' Party (abbreviated in German as NSDAP), commonly referred to in English as the Nazi Party, was a far-right political party in Germany that was active between 1920 and 1945, that created and supported the ideology of National Socialism. Its precursor, the German Workers' Party (Deutsche Arbeiterpartei; DAP), existed from 1919 to 1920. https://en.wikipedia.org/wiki/Nazi_Party

[22] Fritz uses the German proverb "Aus dem Herzen (k)eine Mördergrube machen" meaning 'to speak frankly'

[23] Grünwald - town south of Munich

[24] Reference to 'in das Gebet nehmen' as it is a German proverb meaning (literally 'to include in the prayers') to set strong rules and not to deviate from them

[25] Fritz refers to the girls calling him their 'little patriarch'

[26] Crailsheim - town west of Nuremberg

[27] Mustang planes – Reference to an American WWII war plane type

[28] Striezel - a kind of braided yeast pastry

[29] Freimann – Town that is part of Schwabing in Munich today

[30] Kriegsverdienstkreuz (KVK) - The War Merit Cross (German: Kriegsverdienstkreuz) was a federal decoration of Germany during World War II. By the end of the conflict, it was issued in four degrees and had an equivalent civil award. A "de-Nazified" version of the War Merit Cross was reissued in 1957 by the Bundeswehr for its veterans. https://en.wikipedia.org/wiki/War_Merit_Cross

[31] Olching - town northwest of Munich

[32] Reference to the German folk song 'Das Fluchtlied' written by Ernst Ferdinant August in 1812

[33] Walk to Canossa - Idiomatic phrase with a historical reference to the 'Walk to Canossa' meaning the unavoidable and painful; The Road to Canossa, sometimes called the Walk to Canossa (German: Gang nach Canossa/Kanossa) or Humiliation of Canossa (Italian: L'umiliazione di Canossa), refers to Holy Roman Emperor Henry IV's trek to Canossa Castle, Italy, where Pope Gregory VII was staying as the guest of Margravine Matilda of Tuscany, at the height of the investiture controversy in January 1077 to seek absolution of his excommunication. https://en.wikipedia.org/wiki/Road_to_Canossa

[34] German proverb 'Herz in die Hose fallen' meaning to lose pretty much all hope

[35] Organisation Todt (OT) was a civil and military engineering organization in Nazi Germany from 1933 to 1945, named for its founder, Fritz Todt, an engineer and senior Nazi. The organization was responsible for a huge range of engineering projects both in Nazi Germany and in occupied territories from France to the Soviet Union during World War II. It became notorious for using forced labor. From 1943 until 1945 during the late phase of the Third Reich, OT administered all constructions of concentration camps to supply forced labor to industry. https://en.wikipedia.org/wiki/Organisation_Todt

[36] Military Police (MP) are law enforcement agencies connected with, or part of, the military of a state. https://en.wikipedia.org/wiki/Military_police#United_States

[37] In this context a reference to a toilet

[38] Notgemeinschaft – A group of people that, by fate of life, has been forced to be together for a period of time needing to find ways to support each other.

[39] 'Let's go, let's go' – Not knowing English very well, Fritz rephrasing orders by American soldiers

[40] Idiomatic reference meaning: extremely slowly

[41] Likely a reference to the city Granada in Spain

[42] Fritz realizes that many of his fellow prisoners expected that the Allied forces treat them humanely as POWs by default with some of them actually believing - not knowing better or just ignoring the truth – that prisoners in German camps were treated much better.

[43] PW - Reference to Prisoners of War

[44] Kurt (Häber) – Twin brother of Otto Häber (both older brothers of Fritz), born November 25, 1903 in Leipzig; When Fritz was incarcerated in 1933 and 1934, it was in conjunction with Kurt's activities as a member of the KPD (German Communist Party) charging them with 'overturning the constitutional order by violence'.

[45] Fritz refers to the year 1945

[46] Reference to the end of World War I in 1918

[47] Reference to the German People

[48] Reference to the multi-party parliamentary system of the Weimar Republic

[49] SPD - The Social Democratic Party of Germany (German: Sozialdemokratische Partei Deutschlands, SPD) is a social-democratic political party in Germany that was founded in 1863. https://en.wikipedia.org/wiki/Social_Democratic_Party_of_Germany

[50] KPD - The Communist Party of Germany (German: Kommunistische Partei Deutschlands, KPD) was a major political party in the Weimar Republic between 1918 and 1933, an underground resistance movement in Nazi Germany, and a minor party in West Germany in the postwar period until it was banned in 1956. https://en.wikipedia.org/wiki/Communist_Party_of_Germany

[51] U.K. - Unabkömmlichstellung und Zurückstellung (exemption from military service and deferment) https://de.wikipedia.org/wiki/Unabk%C3%B6mmlichstellung_(UK)_und_Zur%C3%BCckstellung

[52] German proverb "Ein Blaues Wunder erleben' meaning an unexpected brutal treatment or the shock of my life or an unexpected turn of events, etc.

[53] Presumably a reference to a German grinding machine manufacturer. Fritz however uses it as a metaphor to describe the extreme harsh training methods of his superiors ('jemanden schleifen').

[54] VR – It is likely that the intent was to train Fritz to become a "Horcher" at his anti-air-craft gun and searchlight unit for him to 'listen' for approaching enemy planes using radar equipment.

[55] U.A. Überprüfungslehrgang – Likely a reference to a staff sergeant level rank training course or seminar to test his skills and knowledge having been promoted to such rank.

[56] Lugau - town east of Zwickau

[57] Oelsnitz - town southwest of Zwickau

[58] Der Kämpfer (‹The Fighter›) was a German-language daily newspaper published in the Chemnitz-Zwickau area. Originally a newspaper connected to the Independent Social Democratic Party of Germany (USPD), it became an organ of the Communist Party of Germany in January 1919. The newspaper was suppressed on 2 May, 1919 but reappeared the following year. https://en.wikipedia.org/wiki/Der_K%C3%A4mpfer

[59] The Reichswehr (English: Reich Defense) – a formed military organization of Germany from 1919 until 1935 when it was united with the new Wehrmacht (Defense Force) https://en.wikipedia.org/wiki/Reichswehr

[60] Reference to Hermann Fleissner who was German Social Democratic politician. "In November 1918, during the German Revolution, Fleissner was a member of the Council of the People's Deputies of Saxony. On 10 November 1918, Fleissner declared the Republic of Saxony in the premises of the Circus Sarrasani. He joined the Cabinet of Richard Lipinski as Minister for Military Affairs. He held this office until 16 January 1919. Between 1920 and 1924 he was Minister of State for National Education" https://en.wikipedia.org/wiki/Her-mann_Fleissner

[61] Reference to the Weimar Republic

[62] Friedrich Ebert; 4 February 1871 – 28 February 1925) was a German politician of the Social Democratic Party of Germany (SPD) and the first President of Germany from 1919 until his death in office in 1925. https://en.wikipedia.org/wiki/Friedrich_Ebert

[63] USPD - The Independent Social Democratic Party of Germany (German: Unabhängige Sozialdemokratische Partei Deutschlands, USPD) was a short-lived political party in Germany during the German Empire and the Weimar Republic. The organization was established in 1917 as the result of a split of left-wing members of the Social Democratic Party of

Germany (SPD). The organization attempted to chart a centrist course between electorally oriented revisionism on the one hand and Bolshevism on the other. The organization was terminated in 1931 through merger with the Socialist Workers' Party of Germany (SAPD). https://en.wikipedia.org/wiki/Independent_Social_Democratic_Party_of_Germany

[64] Reference to seats in the German multi-party system parliament in the Weimar Republic at the time

[65] Likely a reference to hosanna meaning "save, rescue, savior"

[66] 'Splitter und Balken' is likely a reference to the bible (Matthew 7:3): "The meaning of this verse is fairly clear. It is an attack on the hypocrites who attack others for their small flaws while ignoring their own massive ones." https://en.wikipedia.org/wiki/Matthew_7:3

[67] Fritz uses the German proverb 'An die eigene Nase fassen' meaning to 'take a good look at yourself in the mirror'

[68] Wilkau - town south of Zwickau

[69] Auto Union AG, Chemnitz, was an amalgamation of four German automobile manufacturers, founded in 1932 and established in 1936 in Chemnitz, Saxony. It is the immediate predecessor of Audi as it is known today. https://en.wikipedia.org/wiki/Auto_Union

[70] The Pfennig (pl. pfennigs or pfennige; symbol Pf. or ₰) or penny is a former German coin or note, which was official currency from the 9th century until the introduction of the euro in 2002. While a valuable coin during the Middle Ages, it lost its value through the years and was the minor coin of the Mark currencies in the German Reich, West and East Germany, and the reunified Germany until the introduction of the euro. Pfennig was also the name of the subunit of the Danzig mark (1922–1923) and the Danzig gulden (1923–1939) in the Free City of Danzig (modern Gdańsk, Poland). https://en.wikipedia.org/wiki/Pfennig

[71] Hulda – Oldest sister of Fritz, born in 1886, who – with her husband - moved to and lived in Brazil in the mid-1920s but returned to Germany in the early 1930s. Her relationship with Meta, mother of Fritz, was often quite strained which only marginally impacted his life.

[72] Fritz refers - in a bit derogatory way - to his master as a 'kleiner Knopf' referring to a person of short height

[73] Roßlau - town north of Leipzig

[74] Rödel-Bach - a creek nearby

[75] Haukenberg - a hill nearby

[76] German proverb 'das Vaterunser durch unsere Backen blasen' meaning that a person is famished and the skin is so thin that one can see the bones through it

[77] Elsterhorst - Today Nardt, a town northwest of Hoyerswerda

[78] Correct spelling is Attichy

[79] Fritz uses the German term 'Filzwiese' as a reference to an outdoor place for officials to conduct a thorough personal examination which might have included delousing efforts

[80] In this context likely a reference to a permanent workforce

[81] 'Zoning Cage' – Likely a reference to designated location/hall to gather as a group

[82] The *Wehrmacht* (lit. 'defense force') was the unified armed forces of Nazi Germany from 1935 to 1945. It consisted of the Heer (army), the Kriegsmarine (navy) and the Luftwaffe (air force). The designation *"Wehrmacht"* replaced the previously-used term Reichswehr, and was the manifestation of the Nazi regime's efforts to rearm Germany to a greater extent than the Treaty of Versailles permitted. https://en.wikipedia.org/wiki/Wehrmacht

[83] Feldgericht - a reference to a local (in the field) court martial institution that was empowered to prosecute and convict German soldiers.

ABOUT THE AUTHOR

BERND, GRANDSON OF FRITZ, WAS born in East Berlin - after the Berlin Wall was erected. He grew up in the German Democratic Republic under a Communist ruling government. Bernd attended the Technische Universität in Chemnitz in Saxony/Germany and graduated with a Master's Degree in Mechanical Engineering, Manufacturing Process Design and Computer Aided Manufacturing. Very early on in his life, he started getting interested in German history, music, and modern information technology. When the Berlin Wall, separating East and West Berlin, fell on November 9 in 1989, his world radically changed – an event that let him embark on a personal journey to eventually move to Phoenix in Arizona where he lives today.

Bernd's move to the United States connects him with Fritz who served many months in an American POW camp in 1945-1946 after WWII ended. The – what could be called: The Häber Family Trilogy – link between him and his grandfather is Bernd's father Herbert Häber who had climbed up in the hierarchy of the East German Communist Party, the SED, and later became a member of the Polit-buro in 1984, the political body composed of the highest officials of the party, state, and security organs. In 1985, Herbert was expelled from the Politburo because of a staged high-power plot against him. After German reunification in 1990, Herbert was indicted and prosecuted for being allegedly responsible, as a Politburo member, for some of the killings at the Berlin Wall. He had to face two related criminal trials at the District Court of Berlin between 1995 and 2004.

Bernd is the author of several books, such as *"Letters To and From My Senators FLAKE and MCCAIN: How they might have failed to fulfill their constitutional obligation"*, *"Tempest - 20th Anniversary"*, and *"The Wondrous Story of Hugo and Matilda"*.

Bernd co-led the Spanish Civil War history project together with Björn Krondorfer - Director, Martin-Springer Institute at the Northern Arizona University called *"Stories from the Spanish Civil War"* which includes Bernd's great uncle (and brother-in-law of Fritz) and other International Brigades volunteers from the United States, the UK and Canada.

Bernd currently works on his father's life story & history under the working title *"Koalition der Vernunft"* (Coalition of Sanity).

Bernd is the founder of Worldstrings Promotion – a music agency with a mission to *Keep bringing People together through the Power of Music.*

Printed in the USA
CPSIA information can be obtained
at www.ICGtesting.com
JSHW011519100324
58909JS00006B/27